# The New

# Keto Diet

## Cookbook for Beginners

**2000** Days of Easy & Yummy Ketogenic Recipes for Beginners With 30-Day Meal Plan, Low Carb & Low Sugar Delicious Meals To Help Control Weight

*Debra D. Morgan*

# CONTENTS

# INTRODUCTION

Debra D. Morgan is a passionate advocate for healthy living and a seasoned culinary expert. With over a decade of experience in the world of nutrition and dietetics, she has dedicated her career to helping individuals achieve their health and wellness goals. Debra holds a Bachelor's degree in Nutrition Science from a leading university and is a certified dietitian and nutritionist.

Her journey towards writing the Keto Diet Cookbook began with her fascination for the ketogenic diet's transformative effects on people's lives. As an accomplished chef and nutritionist, she embarked on a comprehensive research and recipe development process to create a collection of delicious, easy-to-follow keto recipes that cater to various tastes and dietary preferences.

Debra's passion for promoting balanced, sustainable, and health-focused eating shines through in her cookbook. Her background in clinical nutrition and hands-on culinary experience allows her to offer valuable insights into the Keto Diet's practical implementation and its potential benefits. Debra's aim is to empower readers to embrace a healthier lifestyle through flavorful, keto-friendly meals while demystifying the diet's complexities.

When she's not crafting nutritious recipes or sharing her expertise in nutrition seminars, Debra enjoys exploring new culinary trends, traveling, and spending quality time with her family. Her Keto Diet Cookbook is the culmination of her dedication to helping individuals achieve their health and wellness aspirations through the power of delicious, keto-approved cuisine.

# Getting to know keto diet

The ketogenic diet, commonly known as the "keto diet," is a low-carbohydrate, high-fat diet designed to shift the body's metabolism into a state known as ketosis. Ketosis is a natural metabolic state in which the body primarily uses fat rather than carbohydrates for fuel.

**Macronutrient Composition:** About 70-80% of daily calories come from fat, 15-20% from protein, and only 5-10% from carbohydrates.

**Carbohydrate restriction:** Carbohydrate intake is restricted to a very low level, usually about 20-50 grams of net carbohydrates per day.

**Emphasize Fats:** Encourage the consumption of healthy fats such as avocados, nuts, seeds, olive oil and fatty fish. Saturated and trans fats are usually limited.

**Moderate protein intake:** Protein intake should be moderate and controlled to prevent excess protein from being converted to glucose, which can disrupt ketosis. Sources of protein include meat, poultry, fish, dairy products and plant foods.

# How does the Keto Diet work?

**Step 1: Carbohydrate Restriction**

The diet begins with a drastic reduction in carbohydrate intake (20-50g/day).

**Step 2: Glycogen Depletion**

Reduced carbs lead to the depletion of glycogen (stored glucose) in the liver and muscles.

**Step 3: Ketosis Initiation**

With low glycogen, the liver starts converting fats into ketones for energy.

**Step 4: Ketone Utilization**

The body uses ketones for energy, including the brain.

**Step 5: Fatty Acid Oxidation**

Fat stores are broken down and used for energy.

### Step 6: Satiety

Higher fat and protein content can reduce appetite and calorie intake.

### Step 7: Weight Loss

The body's reliance on fat stores can lead to weight loss.

### Step 8: Steady Blood Sugar

Fewer carbs result in more stable blood sugar levels.

### Step 9: Metabolic Adaptation

The body becomes efficient at using fat for energy over time.

## Benefits of the Keto Diet

### WEIGHT LOSS

The primary reason people adopt the Keto Diet is for weight loss. By reducing carbohydrate intake and shifting the body into ketosis, where it burns fat for energy, individuals may experience significant and sustained weight loss.

### IMPROVED BLOOD SUGAR CONTROL

The Keto Diet can lead to stabilized blood sugar levels, making it particularly beneficial for people with diabetes or those at risk of developing type 2 diabetes. By reducing carbohydrate intake, there's less demand for insulin, potentially improving insulin sensitivity.

## REDUCED APPETITE

The higher fat and protein content of the Keto Diet can help reduce appetite and curb cravings. Many individuals report feeling less hungry while following the diet, making it easier to control calorie intake.

## INCREASED ENERGY LEVELS

Some people on the Keto Diet report experiencing consistent energy levels throughout the day. This may be attributed to the steady supply of energy from fat stores.

## IMPROVED FOCUS AND MENTAL CLARITY

While more research is needed in this area, some individuals claim to experience improved cognitive function, focus, and reduced brain fog while on the Keto Diet.

## BETTER BLOOD LIPID PROFILE

Studies suggest that the Keto Diet can lead to favorable changes in blood lipid profiles by increasing high-density lipoprotein (HDL) or "good" cholesterol levels and reducing triglycerides. However, its impact on low-density lipoprotein (LDL) or "bad" cholesterol can vary among individuals.

## REDUCED INFLAMMATION

Some studies indicate that the Keto Diet may have anti-inflammatory effects, which could be beneficial for individuals with conditions related to chronic inflammation.

# Frequently asked questions about Keto Diet

**1. Is the Keto Diet safe?**

While generally considered safe for most, it may not be suitable for everyone. Consult a healthcare professional before starting, especially if you have underlying health conditions.

**2. What can I eat on the Keto Diet?**

You can consume foods rich in healthy fats (avocado, nuts), moderate protein (meat, fish), and low-carb vegetables. Foods high in carbohydrates (sugar, grains) are limited.

**3. Are there any risks or drawbacks?**

Risks may include the "keto flu" during the initial phase, nutrient deficiencies if not balanced, and potential side effects. Long-term effects are still being studied.

**4. Can I do the Keto Diet as a vegetarian or vegan?**

Yes, with careful planning. Focus on plant-based fats and protein sources while minimizing carbs.

**5. How do I start the Keto Diet?**

Begin by calculating your macronutrient ratios, planning keto-friendly meals, and gradually reducing carb intake. Monitoring ketosis with test strips may help.

**6. What is the "keto flu"?**

The "keto flu" refers to temporary symptoms like fatigue, headaches, and irritability during the initial adaptation phase. Staying hydrated and getting electrolytes can help.

**7. How long should I follow the Keto Diet?**

The duration varies by individual goals. Some use it short-term for weight loss, while others adopt it as a long-term lifestyle.

# 30-DAY MEAL PLAN

| DAY | Breakfast | Lunch | Dinner |
|---|---|---|---|
| 1 | Tofu Stuffed Peppers 15 | Mushroom Beef Ste 37 | Easy Asian Chicken 52 |
| 2 | Cheddar Cheese Chip 16 | Pork Osso Bucc 37 | Chicken And Bacon Rolls 52 |
| 3 | Spicy Chicken Cucumber Bite 16 | Baked Pork Meatballs In Pasta Sauce 38 | Turkey & Cheese Stuffed Mushrooms 52 |
| 4 | Spinach Turnip Salad With Baco 16 | Pork Burgers With Caramelized Onion Rings 38 | Chicken With Monterey Jack Cheese 53 |
| 5 | Spiced Gruyere Crisp 17 | Ground Beef And Cabbage Stir Fry 39 | Homemade Chicken Pizza Calzone 53 |
| 6 | Jalapeno Popper Sprea 17 | Chuck Roast Beef 39 | Yummy Chicken Nuggets 54 |
| 7 | Walnut Butter On Cracke 18 | Beef Skewers With Ranch Dressing 39 | Roasted Garlic Lemon Dip 82 |
| 8 | Cheese-jalapeno Mushroom 18 | Hot Pork With Dill Pickles 40 | Dijon Vinaigrette 82 |
| 9 | Pesto Stuffed Mushroom 19 | Zucchini Boats With Beef And Pimiento Rojo 40 | Avocado-lime Crema 82 |
| 10 | Old Bay Chicken Wing 20 | Cherry-balsamic Sauced Beef 40 | Caesar Dressing 83 |
| 11 | Garlic Flavored Kale Tater 20 | Adobo Beef Fajitas 41 | Keto Thousand Island Dressing 83 |
| 12 | Dill Pickles With Tuna-mayo Toppin 20 | Beef And Cabbage With Spice Packet 41 | Tzatziki 83 |
| 13 | Sautéed Brussels Sprout 21 | Jalapeno Beef Pot Roasted 41 | Almond-crusted Chicken Breasts 56 |
| 14 | Coconut And Chocolate Bar 21 | Dr. Pepper Pulled Pork 42 | Heart Healthy Chicken Salad 56 |
| 15 | Parmesan Cracker 22 | Beef Cauliflower Curry 42 | Chicken, Broccoli & Cashew Stir-fry 57 |

| DAY | Breakfast | Lunch | Dinner |
|---|---|---|---|
| 16 | Butternut And Kale Sou 26 | Classic Italian Bolognese Sauce 42 | Chicken With Parmesan Topping 57 |
| 17 | Balsamic Cucumber Sala 26 | Cranberry Gravy Brisket 43 | Halibut With Pesto 70 |
| 18 | Green Salad With Bacon And Blue Chees 27 | Italian Sausage Stew 43 | Avocado Tuna Boats 70 |
| 19 | Green Minestrone Sou 27 | White Wine Lamb Chops 43 | Enchilada Sauce On Mahi Mahi 70 |
| 20 | Mushroom-broccoli Sou 28 | New York Strip Steak With Mushroom Sauce 44 | Chipotle Salmon Asparagus 71 |
| 21 | Chicken Creamy Sou 28 | Pork Casserole 44 | Bang Bang Shrimps 71 |
| 22 | Sour Cream And Cucumber 29 | Paprika Pork Chops 45 | Baked Salmon With Pistachio Crust 71 |
| 23 | Green Sala 30 | Creamy Pork Chops 45 | Steamed Chili-rubbed Tilapia 72 |
| 24 | Mushroom Sou 30 | Beef And Feta Salad 45 | Steamed Herbed Red Snapper 72 |
| 25 | Herb Butter With Parsle 60 | Habanero And Beef Balls 46 | Flounder With Dill And Capers 72 |
| 26 | Grilled Parmesan Eggplan 60 | Mustard-lemon Beef 46 | Brownies With Coco Milk 90 |
| 27 | Sriracha Tofu With Yogurt Sauc 60 | Chicken In Creamy Mushroom Sauce 49 | Almond Milk Hot Chocolate 90 |
| 28 | Keto Enchilada Bak 61 | Chicken Pesto 49 | Fast 'n Easy Cookie In A Mug 90 |
| 29 | Roasted Brussels Sprouts With Sunflower Seed 61 | Oven-baked Skillet Lemon Chicken 49 | Spicy Cheese Crackers 91 |
| 30 | Grated Cauliflower With Seasoned May 61 | Easy Chicken Meatloaf 50 | Mint Chocolate Protein Shake 91 |

# Appetizers, Snacks & Side Dishes

# Appetizers, Snacks & Side Dishes

## Cobb Salad With Blue Cheese Dressing

Servings: 6

Cooking Time: 2 Hours 40 Minutes

**Ingredients:**

- ½ cup buttermilk
- 1 cup mayonnaise
- 2 tbsp sugar-free Worcestershire sauce
- ½ cup sour cream
- 1 ½ cup crumbled blue cheese
- Salt and black pepper to taste
- 2 tbsp chopped chives
- 6 eggs
- 1 cup water
- Ice bath
- 2 chicken breasts, boneless and skinless
- Salt and black pepper to taste
- 5 strips bacon
- 1 iceberg lettuce, cut into chunks
- 1 romaine lettuce, chopped
- 1 bibb lettuce, cored and leaves removed
- 2 avocado, pitted and diced
- 2 large tomatoes, chopped
- ½ cup crumbled blue cheese
- 2 scallions, chopped

**Directions:**

1. In a bowl, whisk the buttermilk, mayonnaise, Worcestershire sauce, and sour cream. Stir in the blue cheese, salt, pepper, and chives. Place in the refrigerator to chill for 2 hours.
2. Bring the eggs to boil in salted water over medium heat for 10 minutes. Once ready, drain the eggs and transfer to the ice bath. Peel and chop the eggs. Set aside.
3. Preheat the grill pan over high heat. Season the chicken with salt and pepper. Grill for 3 minutes on each side. Remove to a plate to cool for 3 minutes, and cut into bite-size chunks.
4. Fry the bacon in another pan set over medium heat until crispy, about 6 minutes. Remove, let cool for 2 minutes, and chop.
5. Arrange the lettuce leaves in a salad bowl and in single piles, add the avocado, tomatoes, eggs, bacon, and chicken. Sprinkle the blue cheese over the salad as well as the scallions and black pepper.
6. Drizzle the blue cheese dressing on the salad and serve with low carb bread.

**Nutrition Info:**

- Info Per Servings 2g Carbs, 23g Protein, 14g Fat, 122 Calories

## Tofu Stuffed Peppers

Servings: 8

Cooking Time: 10 Minutes

**Ingredients:**

- 1 package firm tofu, crumbled
- 1 onion, finely chopped
- ½ teaspoon turmeric powder
- 1 teaspoon coriander powder
- 8 banana peppers, top-end sliced and seeded
- Salt and pepper to taste
- 3 tablespoons oil

**Directions:**

1. Preheat oven to 400oF.
2. In a mixing bowl, combine the tofu, onion, coconut oil, turmeric powder, red chili powder, coriander powder, and salt. Mix until well-combined.
3. Scoop the tofu mixture into the hollows of the banana peppers.
4. Place the stuffed peppers in one layer in a lightly greased baking sheet.
5. Cook for 10 minutes.
6. Serve and enjoy.

**Nutrition Info:**

- Info Per Servings 4.1g Carbs, 1.2g Protein, 15.6g Fat, 187 Calories

# Cheddar Cheese Chips

Servings: 4

Cooking Time: 8 Minutes

**Ingredients:**

- 8 oz cheddar cheese or provolone cheese or Edam cheese, in slices
- ½ tsp paprika powder

**Directions:**

1. Line baking sheet with foil and preheat oven to 400F.
2. Place cheese slices on a baking sheet and sprinkle the paprika powder on top.
3. Pop in the oven and bake for 8 to 10 minutes.
4. Pay an attention when the timer reaches 6 to 7 minutes as a burnt cheese tastes bitter.
5. Serve and enjoy.

**Nutrition Info:**

- Info Per Servings 2.0g Carbs, 13.0g Protein, 19.0g Fat, 228 Calories

# Spicy Chicken Cucumber Bites

Servings: 6

Cooking Time: 5 Minutes

**Ingredients:**

- 2 cucumbers, sliced with a 3-inch thickness
- 2 cups small dices leftover chicken
- ¼ jalapeño pepper, seeded and minced
- 1 tbsp Dijon mustard
- ⅓ cup mayonnaise
- Salt and black pepper to taste

**Directions:**

1. Cut mid-level holes in cucumber slices with a knife and set aside. Combine chicken, jalapeno pepper, mustard, mayonnaise, salt, and black pepper to be evenly mixed. Fill cucumber holes with chicken mixture and serve.

**Nutrition Info:**

- Info Per Servings 0g Carbs, 10g Protein, 14g Fat, 170 Calories

# Spinach Turnip Salad With Bacon

Servings: 4

Cooking Time: 40 Minutes

**Ingredients:**

- 6 turnips, cut into wedges
- 1 tsp olive oil
- 1 cup baby spinach chopped
- 3 radishes, sliced
- 3 bacon slices, sliced
- 4 tbsp sour cream
- 2 tsp mustard seeds
- 1 tsp Dijon mustard
- 1 tbsp red wine vinegar
- Salt and black pepper to taste
- 1 tbsp chopped chives

**Directions:**

1. Preheat the oven to 400°F. Line a baking sheet with parchment paper, toss the turnips with pepper, drizzle with the olive oil, and bake for 25 minutes, turning halfway. Let cool.
2. Spread the baby spinach in the bottom of a salad bowl and top with the radishes. Remove the turnips to the salad bowl. Fry the bacon in a skillet over medium heat until crispy, about 5 minutes.
3. Mix the sour cream, mustard seeds, Dijon mustard, vinegar, and salt with the bacon. Add a little water to deglaze the bottom of the skillet and turn off the heat.
4. Pour the bacon mixture over the vegetables, scatter the chives over it, and season with black pepper.Serve the salad with grilled pork chops.

**Nutrition Info:**

- Info Per Servings 3.1g Carbs, 9.5g Protein, 18.3g Fat, 193 Calories

# Spiced Gruyere Crisps

Servings: 4

Cooking Time: 10 Minutes

**Ingredients:**

- 2 cups gruyere cheese, shredded
- ½ tsp garlic powder
- ¼ tsp onion powder
- 1 rosemary sprig, minced
- ½ tsp chili powder

**Directions:**

1. Set oven to 400ºF. Coat two baking sheets with parchment paper.
2. Mix Gruyere cheese with the seasonings. Take 1 tablespoon of cheese mixture and form small mounds on the baking sheets. Bake for 6 minutes. Leave to cool. Serve.

**Nutrition Info:**

- Info Per Servings 2.9g Carbs, 14.5g Protein, 15g Fat, 205 Calories

# Jalapeno Popper Spread

Servings: 8

Cooking Time: 3 Mins

**Ingredients:**

- 2 packages cream cheese, softened; low-carb
- 1 cup. mayonnaise
- 1 can chopped green chilies, drained
- 2 ounces canned diced jalapeno peppers, drained
- 1 cup. grated Parmesan cheese

**Directions:**

1. Combine cream cheese and mayonnaise in a bowl until incorporated. Add in jalapeno peppers and green chilies. In a microwave safe bowl, spread jalapeno peppers mixture and sprinkle with Parmesan cheese.
2. Microwave jalapeno peppers mixture on High about 3 minutes or until warm.

**Nutrition Info:**

- Info Per Servings 1g Carbs, 2.1g Protein, 11.1g Fat, 110 Calories

# Bacon-flavored Kale Chips

Servings: 6

Cooking Time: 25 Minutes

**Ingredients:**

- 2 tbsp butter
- ¼ cup bacon grease
- 1-lb kale, around 1 bunch
- 1 to 2 tsp salt

**Directions:**

1. Remove the rib from kale leaves and tear it into 2-inch pieces.
2. Clean the kale leaves thoroughly and dry them inside a salad spinner.
3. In a skillet, add the butter to the bacon grease and warm the two fats under low heat. Add salt and stir constantly.
4. Set aside and let it cool.
5. Put the dried kale in a Ziploc back and add the cool liquid bacon grease and butter mixture.
6. Seal the Ziploc back and gently shake the kale leaves with the butter mixture. The leaves should have this shiny consistency, which means that they are coated evenly with the fat.
7. Pour the kale leaves on a cookie sheet and sprinkle more salt if necessary.
8. Bake for 25 minutes inside a preheated 350oF oven or until the leaves start to turn brown as well as crispy.

**Nutrition Info:**

- Info Per Servings 6.6g Carbs, 3.3g Protein, 13.1g Fat, 148 Calories

# Walnut Butter On Cracker

Servings: 1

Cooking Time: 0 Minutes

**Ingredients:**

- 1 tablespoon walnut butter
- 2 pieces Mary's gone crackers

**Directions:**

1. Spread ½ tablespoon of walnut butter per cracker and enjoy.

**Nutrition Info:**

- Info Per Servings 4.0g Carbs, 1.0g Protein, 14.0g Fat, 134 Calories

# Cheese-jalapeno Mushrooms

Servings: 8

Cooking Time: 20 Mins

**Ingredients:**

- 2 slices bacon
- 1 package cream cheese, softened; low-carb
- 3 tablespoons shredded Cheddar cheese
- 1 jalapeno pepper, ribs and seeds removed, finely chopped
- 8 mushrooms, stems removed and chopped and caps reserved; keto-friendly
- Salt and pepper to taste
- Cooking spray

**Directions:**

1. Preheat the oven to 400 degrees F.
2. In a large bowl, combine bacon, cream cheese, cheese, jalapenos, salt and pepper. Mix well.
3. Spoon the bacon filling into each mushroom cap. Then transfer the stuffed mushroom caps to a baking dish or sheet sprayed with cooking spray.
4. Bake until the mushroom caps are cooked, about 15-20 minutes.
5. Serve and enjoy.

**Nutrition Info:**

- Info Per Servings 2.5g Carbs, 6.1g Protein, 13.4g Fat, 151 Calories

# Pecorino-mushroom Balls

Servings: 4

Cooking Time: 20 Minutes

**Ingredients:**

- 2 tbsp butter, softened
- 2 garlic cloves, minced
- 2 cups portobello mushrooms, chopped
- 4 tbsp blanched almond flour
- 4 tbsp ground flax seeds
- 4 tbsp hemp seeds
- 4 tbsp sunflower seeds
- 1 tbsp cajun seasonings
- 1 tsp mustard
- 2 eggs, whisked
- ½ cup pecorino cheese

**Directions:**

1. Set a pan over medium-high heat and warm 1 tablespoon of butter. Add in mushrooms and garlic and sauté until there is no more water in mushrooms.
2. Place in pecorino cheese, almond flour, hemp seeds, mustard, eggs, sunflower seeds, flax seeds, and Cajun seasonings. Create 4 burgers from the mixture.
3. In a pan, warm the remaining butter; fry the burgers for 7 minutes. Flip them over with a wide spatula and cook for 6 more minutes. Serve while warm.

**Nutrition Info:**

- Info Per Servings 7.7g Carbs, 16.8g Protein, 30g Fat, 370 Calories

# Devilled Eggs With Sriracha Mayo

Servings: 4

Cooking Time: 15 Minutes

**Ingredients:**

- 8 large eggs
- 3 cups water
- Ice water bath
- 3 tbsp sriracha sauce
- 4 tbsp mayonnaise
- Salt to taste
- ¼ tsp smoked paprika

**Directions:**

1. Bring eggs to boil in salted water in a pot over high heat, and then reduce the heat to simmer for 10 minutes. Transfer eggs to an ice water bath, let cool completely and peel the shells.
2. Slice the eggs in half height wise and empty the yolks into a bowl. Smash with a fork and mix in sriracha sauce, mayonnaise, and half of the paprika until smooth.
3. Spoon filling into a piping bag with a round nozzle and fill the egg whites to be slightly above the brim. Garnish with remaining paprika and serve immediately.

**Nutrition Info:**

- Info Per Servings 1g Carbs, 4g Protein, 19g Fat, 195 Calories

# Cardamom And Cinnamon Fat Bombs

Servings: 10

Cooking Time: 3 Minutes

**Ingredients:**

- ¼ tsp ground cardamom (green)
- ¼ tsp ground cinnamon
- ½ cup unsweetened shredded coconut
- ½ tsp vanilla extract
- 3-oz unsalted butter, room temperature

**Directions:**

1. Place a nonstick pan on medium fire and toast coconut until lightly browned.
2. In a bowl, mix all ingredients.
3. Evenly roll into 10 equal balls.
4. Let it cool in the fridge.
5. Serve and enjoy.

**Nutrition Info:**

- Info Per Servings 0.4g Carbs, 0.4g Protein, 10.0g Fat, 90 Calories

# Pesto Stuffed Mushrooms

Servings: 6

Cooking Time: 25 Minutes

**Ingredients:**

- 6 large cremini mushrooms
- 6 bacon slices
- 2 tablespoons basil pesto
- 5 tablespoons low-fat cream cheese softened

**Directions:**

1. Line a cookie sheet with foil and preheat oven to 375oF.
2. In a small bowl mix well, pesto and cream cheese.
3. Remove stems of mushrooms and discard. Evenly fill mushroom caps with pesto-cream cheese filling.
4. Get one stuffed mushroom and a slice of bacon. Wrap the bacon all over the mushrooms. Repeat process on remaining mushrooms and bacon.
5. Place bacon-wrapped mushrooms on prepared pan and bake for 25 minutes or until bacon is crispy.
6. Let it cool, evenly divide into suggested servings, and enjoy.

**Nutrition Info:**

- Info Per Servings 2.0g Carbs, 5.0g Protein, 12.2g Fat, 137.8 Calories

# Old Bay Chicken Wings

Servings: 4

Cooking Time: 30 Minutes

**Ingredients:**

- 3 pounds chicken wings
- ¾ cup almond flour
- 1 tablespoon old bay spices
- 1 teaspoon lemon juice, freshly squeezed
- ½ cup butter
- Salt and pepper to taste

**Directions:**

1. Preheat oven to 400oF.
2. In a mixing bowl, combine all ingredients except for the butter.
3. Place in an even layer in a baking sheet.
4. Bake for 30 minutes. Halfway through the cooking time, shake the fryer basket for even cooking.
5. Once cooked, drizzle with melted butter.

**Nutrition Info:**

- Info Per Servings 1.6g Carbs, 52.5g Protein, 59.2g Fat, 700 Calories

# Dill Pickles With Tuna-mayo Topping

Servings: 12

Cooking Time: 40 Minutes

**Ingredients:**

- 18 ounces canned and drained tuna
- 6 large dill pickles
- ¼ tsp garlic powder
- ⅓ cup sugar-free mayonnaise
- 1 tbsp onion flakes

**Directions:**

1. Combine the mayonnaise, tuna, onion flakes, and garlic powder in a bowl. Cut the pickles in half lengthwise. Top each half with tuna mixture. Place in the fridge for 30 minutes before serving.

**Nutrition Info:**

- Info Per Servings 1.5g Carbs, 11g Protein, 10g Fat, 118 Calories

# Garlic Flavored Kale Taters

Servings: 4

Cooking Time: 20 Minutes

**Ingredients:**

- 4 cups kale, rinsed and chopped
- 2 cups cauliflower florets, finely chopped
- 2 tbsp almond milk
- 1 clove of garlic, minced
- 3 tablespoons oil
- 1/8 teaspoon black pepper
- cooking spray

**Directions:**

1. Heat oil in a large skillet and sauté the garlic for 2 minutes. Add the kale until it wilts. Transfer to a large bowl.
2. Add the almond milk. Season with pepper to taste.
3. Evenly divide into 4 and form patties.
4. Lightly grease a baking pan with cooking spray. Place patties on pan. Place pan on the top rack of the oven and broil on low for 6 minutes. Turnover patties and cook for another 4 minutes.
5. Serve and enjoy.

**Nutrition Info:**

- Info Per Servings 5g Carbs, 2g Protein, 11g Fat, 117 Calories

# Sautéed Brussels Sprouts

Servings: 4

Cooking Time: 8 Minutes

**Ingredients:**

- 2 cups Brussels sprouts, halved
- 1 tablespoon balsamic vinegar
- 4 tablespoons olive oil
- Salt and pepper to taste

**Directions:**

1. Place a saucepan on medium-high fire and heat oil for a minute.
2. Add all ingredients and sauté for 7 minutes.
3. Season with pepper and salt.
4. Serve and enjoy.

**Nutrition Info:**

- Info Per Servings 4.6g Carbs, 1.5g Protein, 16.8g Fat, 162 Calories

# Coconut And Chocolate Bars

Servings: 6

Cooking Time: 30 Minutes

**Ingredients:**

- 1 tbsp Stevia
- ¾ cup shredded coconut, unsweetened
- ½ cup ground nuts (almonds, pecans, or walnuts)
- ¼ cup unsweetened cocoa powder
- 4 tbsp coconut oil
- Done

**Directions:**

1. In a medium bowl, mix shredded coconut, nuts, and cocoa powder.
2. Add Stevia and coconut oil.
3. Mix batter thoroughly.
4. In a 9x9 square inch pan or dish, press the batter and for a 30-minutes place in the freezer.
5. Serve and enjoy.

**Nutrition Info:**

- Info Per Servings 2.3g Carbs, 1.6g Protein, 17.8g Fat, 200 Calories

# Nutty Avocado Crostini With Nori

Servings: 4

Cooking Time: 12 Minutes

**Ingredients:**

- 8 slices low carb baguette
- 4 nori sheets
- 1 cup mashed avocado
- ⅓ tsp salt
- 1 tsp lemon juice
- 1 ½ tbsp coconut oil
- ⅓ cup chopped raw walnuts
- 1 tbsp chia seeds

**Directions:**

1. In a bowl, flake the nori sheets into the smallest possible pieces.
2. In another bowl, mix the avocado, salt, and lemon juice, and stir in half of the nori flakes. Set aside.
3. Place the baguette on a baking sheet and toast in a broiler on medium heat for 2 minutes, making sure not to burn. Remove the crostini after and brush with coconut oil on both sides.
4. Top each crostini with the avocado mixture and garnish with the chia seeds, chopped walnuts, Serve the snack immediately.

**Nutrition Info:**

- Info Per Servings 2.8g Carbs, 13.7g Protein, 12.2g Fat, 195 Calories

# Easy Baked Parmesan Chips

Servings: 10

Cooking Time: 10 Minutes

**Ingredients:**

- 1 cup grated Parmesan cheese, low fat
- 1 tablespoon olive oil

**Directions:**

1. Lightly grease a cookie sheet and preheat oven to 400°F.
2. Evenly sprinkle parmesan cheese on a cookie sheet into 10 circles. Place them about ½-inch apart.
3. Drizzle with oil
4. Bake until lightly browned and crisped.
5. Let it cool, evenly divide into suggested servings and enjoy.

**Nutrition Info:**

- Info Per Servings 1.4g Carbs, 2.8g Protein, 12.8g Fat, 142 Calories

# Parmesan Crackers

Servings: 6

Cooking Time: 25 Minutes

**Ingredients:**

- 1 ⅓ cups coconut flour
- 1 ¼ cup grated Parmesan cheese
- Salt and black pepper to taste
- 1 tsp garlic powder
- ⅓ cup butter, softened
- ⅓ tsp sweet paprika
- ⅓ cup heavy cream
- Water as needed

**Directions:**

1. Preheat the oven to 350ºF.
2. Mix the coconut flour, parmesan cheese, salt, pepper, garlic powder, and paprika in a bowl. Add in the butter and mix well. Top with the heavy cream and mix again until a smooth, thick mixture has

formed. Add 1 to 2 tablespoon of water at this point, if it is too thick.

3. Place the dough on a cutting board and cover with plastic wrap. Use a rolling pin to spread out the dough into a light rectangle. Cut cracker squares out of the dough and arrange them on a baking sheet without overlapping. Bake for 20 minutes and transfer to a serving bowl after.

**Nutrition Info:**

- Info Per Servings 0.7g Carbs, 5g Protein, 3g Fat, 115 Calories

# Keto "cornbread"

Servings: 8

Cooking Time: 30 Minutes

**Ingredients:**

- 1 ¼ cups coconut milk
- 4 eggs, beaten
- 4 tbsp baking powder
- ½ cup almond meal
- 3 tablespoons olive oil

**Directions:**

1. Prepare 8 x 8-inch baking dish or a black iron skillet then add shortening.
2. Put the baking dish or skillet inside the oven on 425oF and leave there for 10 minutes.
3. In a bowl, add coconut milk and eggs then mix well. Stir in the rest of the ingredients.
4. Once all ingredients are mixed, pour the mixture into the heated skillet.
5. Then cook for 15 to 20 minutes in the oven until golden brown.

**Nutrition Info:**

- Info Per Servings 2.6g Carbs, 5.4g Protein, 18.9g Fat, 196 Calories

# Soy Garlic Mushrooms

Servings: 8

Cooking Time: 10 Minutes

**Ingredients:**

- 2 pounds mushrooms, sliced
- 3 tablespoons olive oil
- 2 cloves of garlic, minced
- ¼ cup coconut aminos
- 4 tablespoons butter
- Salt and pepper to taste

**Directions:**

1. Place all ingredients in a dish except for the butter and mix until well-combined.
2. Allow marinating for 2 hours in the fridge.
3. In a large saucepan on medium fire, melt the butter and add mushrooms and sauté for 8 minutes. Season with pepper and salt to taste.
4. Serve and enjoy.

**Nutrition Info:**

- Info Per Servings 4.7g Carbs, 3.8g Protein, 11.9g Fat, 152 Calories

# Air Fryer Garlic Chicken Wings

Servings: 4

Cooking Time: 25 Minutes

**Ingredients:**

- 16 pieces chicken wings
- ¾ cup almond flour
- 4 tablespoons minced garlic
- ¼ cup butter, melted
- 2 tablespoons Stevia powder
- Salt and pepper to taste

**Directions:**

1. Preheat oven to 400oF.
2. In a mixing bowl, combine the chicken wings, almond flour, Stevia powder, and garlic. Season with salt and pepper to taste.
3. Place in a lightly greased cookie sheet in an even layer and cook for 25 minutes.
4. Halfway through the cooking time, turnover chicken.
5. Once cooked, place in a bowl and drizzle with melted butter. Toss to coat.
6. Serve and enjoy.

**Nutrition Info:**

- Info Per Servings 7.8g Carbs, 23.7g Protein, 26.9g Fat, 365 Calories

# French Fried Butternut Squash

Servings: 6

Cooking Time: 20 Minutes

**Ingredients:**

- 1 medium butternut squash
- 1 tablespoon chopped fresh thyme
- 1 tablespoon chopped fresh rosemary
- 4 tablespoons olive oil
- 1/2 teaspoon salt
- Cooking spray

**Directions:**

1. Heat oven to 425oF. Lightly coat a baking sheet with cooking spray.
2. Peel skin from butternut squash and cut into even sticks, about 1/2-inch-wide and 3 inches long.
3. In a medium bowl, combine the squash, oil, thyme, rosemary, and salt; mix until the squash is evenly coated.
4. Spread onto the baking sheet and roast for 10 minutes.
5. Remove the baking sheet from the oven and shake to loosen the squash.
6. Return to oven and continue to roast for 10 minutes or until golden brown.
7. Serve and enjoy.

**Nutrition Info:**

- Info Per Servings 1g Carbs, 1g Protein, 9g Fat, 86 Calories

# Cheesy Lettuce Rolls

Servings: 6

Cooking Time: 10 Minutes

**Ingredients:**

- ½ pound gouda cheese, grated
- ½ pound feta cheese, crumbled
- 1 tsp taco seasoning mix
- 2 tbsp olive oil
- 1 ½ cups guacamole
- 1 cup buttermilk
- A head lettuce

**Directions:**

1. Mix both types of cheese with taco seasoning mix. Set pan over medium heat and warm olive oil. Spread the shredded cheese mixture all over the pan. Fry for 5 minutes, turning once.
2. Arrange some of the cheese mixture on each lettuce leaf, top with buttermilk and guacamole, then roll up, folding in the ends to secure and serve.

**Nutrition Info:**

- Info Per Servings 4.9g Carbs, 19.5g Protein, 30g Fat, 370 Calories

# Zucchini And Cheese Gratin

Servings: 8

Cooking Time: 15 Minutes

**Ingredients:**

- 5 tablespoons butter
- 1 onion, sliced
- ½ cup heavy cream
- 4 cups raw zucchini, sliced
- 1 ½ cups shredded pepper Jack cheese
- Salt and pepper to taste

**Directions:**

1. Place all ingredients in a mixing bowl and give a good stir to incorporate everything.
2. Pour the mixture in a heat-proof baking dish.
3. Place in a 350F preheated oven and bake for 15 minutes.
4. Serve and enjoy.

**Nutrition Info:**

- Info Per Servings 5.0g Carbs, 8.0g Protein, 20.0g Fat, 280 Calories

# Middle Eastern Style Tuna Salad

Servings: 6

Cooking Time: 0 Minutes

**Ingredients:**

- ¼ cup chopped pitted ripe olives
- ¼ cup drained and chopped roasted red peppers
- 2 green onions, sliced
- 2 pcs of 6-oz cans of tuna in water, drained and flaked
- 6 cups salad greens like lettuce
- ¼ cup Mayonnaise

**Directions:**

1. Except for salad greens, mix all the ingredients in a bowl.
2. Arrange salad greens on the bottom of the bowl and top with tuna mixture.
3. Serve and enjoy.

**Nutrition Info:**

- Info Per Servings 3g Carbs, 3g Protein, 8g Fat, 92 Calories

# Soups, Stew & Salads

# Soups, Stew & Salads

## Butternut And Kale Soup

Servings: 10

Cooking Time: 30 Minutes

### Ingredients:

- 1 package Italian turkey sausage links, casings removed
- ½ medium butternut squash, peeled and cubed
- 2 cartons reduced-sodium chicken broth
- 1 bunch kale, trimmed and coarsely chopped
- 1/2 cup shaved Parmesan cheese
- 6 tablespoons butter
- Water
- Salt to taste

### Directions:

1. In a stockpot, cook sausage over medium heat until no longer pink, breaking into crumbles, 8-10 minutes.
2. Add squash and broth; bring to a boil. Gradually stir in kale, allowing it to wilt slightly between additions. Return to a boil.
3. Reduce heat; simmer, uncovered, until vegetables are tender, 15-20 minutes. Top servings with cheese.

### Nutrition Info:

- Info Per Servings 5.3g Carbs, 13g Protein, 5g Fat, 118 Calories

## Clam Chowder

Servings: 5

Cooking Time: 10 Minutes

### Ingredients:

- 1 can condensed cream of celery soup, undiluted
- 2 cups half-and-half cream
- 2 cans minced/chopped clams, drained
- 1/4 teaspoon ground nutmeg

- 5 tablespoons butter
- Pepper to taste

### Directions:

1. In a large saucepan, combine all ingredients. Cook and stir over medium heat until heated through.

### Nutrition Info:

- Info Per Servings 3.8g Carbs, 10g Protein, 14g Fat, 251 Calories

## Balsamic Cucumber Salad

Servings: 6

Cooking Time: 0 Minutes

### Ingredients:

- 1 large English cucumber, halved and sliced
- 1 cup grape tomatoes, halved
- 1 medium red onion, sliced thinly
- ¼ cup balsamic vinaigrette
- ¾ cup feta cheese
- Salt and pepper to taste
- ¼ cup olive oil

### Directions:

1. Place all ingredients in a bowl.
2. Toss to coat everything with the dressing.
3. Allow chilling before serving.

### Nutrition Info:

- Info Per Servings 9g Carbs, 4.8g Protein, 16.7g Fat, 253 Calories

# Green Salad With Bacon And Blue Cheese

Servings: 4

Cooking Time: 15 Minutes

**Ingredients:**

- 2 pack mixed salad greens
- 8 strips bacon
- 1 ½ cups crumbled blue cheese
- 1 tbsp white wine vinegar
- 3 tbsp extra virgin olive oil
- Salt and black pepper to taste

**Directions:**

1. Pour the salad greens in a salad bowl; set aside. Fry bacon strips in a skillet over medium heat for 6 minutes, until browned and crispy. Chop the bacon and scatter over the salad. Add in half of the cheese, toss and set aside.
2. In a small bowl, whisk the white wine vinegar, olive oil, salt, and black pepper until dressing is well combined. Drizzle half of the dressing over the salad, toss, and top with remaining cheese. Divide salad into four plates and serve with crusted chicken fries along with remaining dressing.

**Nutrition Info:**

- Info Per Servings 2g Carbs, 4g Protein, 20g Fat, 205 Calories

# Brussels Sprouts Salad With Pecorino Romano

Servings: 6

Cooking Time: 35 Minutes

**Ingredients:**

- 2 lb Brussels sprouts, halved
- 3 tbsp olive oil
- Salt and black pepper to taste
- 2 ½ tbsp balsamic vinegar
- ¼ red cabbage, shredded
- 1 tbsp Dijon mustard
- 1 cup pecorino romano cheese, grated

**Directions:**

1. Preheat oven to 400ºF and line a baking sheet with foil. Toss the brussels sprouts with olive oil, a little salt, black pepper, and balsamic vinegar, in a bowl, and spread on the baking sheet in an even layer. Bake until tender on the inside and crispy on the outside, about 20 to 25 minutes.
2. Transfer to a salad bowl and add the red cabbage, Dijon mustard and half of the cheese. Mix until well combined. Sprinkle with the remaining cheese, share the salad onto serving plates, and serve with syrup-grilled salmon.

**Nutrition Info:**

- Info Per Servings 6g Carbs, 4g Protein, 18g Fat, 210 Calories

# Green Minestrone Soup

Servings: 4

Cooking Time: 25 Minutes

**Ingredients:**

- 2 tbsp ghee
- 2 tbsp onion garlic puree
- 2 heads broccoli, cut in florets
- 2 stalks celery, chopped
- 5 cups vegetable broth
- 1 cup baby spinach
- Salt and black pepper to taste

**Directions:**

1. Melt the ghee in a saucepan over medium heat and sauté the garlic for 3 minutes until softened. Mix in the broccoli and celery, and cook for 4 minutes until slightly tender. Pour in the broth, bring to a boil, then reduce the heat to medium-low and simmer covered for about 5 minutes.
2. Drop in the spinach to wilt, adjust the seasonings, and cook for 4 minutes. Ladle soup into serving bowls. Serve with a sprinkle of grated Gruyere cheese and freshly baked low carb carrot bread.

**Nutrition Info:**

- Info Per Servings 2g Carbs, 8g Protein, 20.3g Fat, 227 Calories

# Mushroom-broccoli Soup

Servings: 4

Cooking Time: 20 Minutes

**Ingredients:**

- 1 onion, diced
- 3 cloves of garlic, diced
- 2 cups mushrooms, chopped
- 2 heads of broccoli, cut into florets
- 1 cup full-fat milk
- 3 cups water
- Pepper and salt to taste

**Directions:**

1. Place a heavy-bottomed pot on medium-high fire and heat for 3 minutes.
2. Add onion, garlic, water, and broccoli. Season generously with pepper and salt.
3. Cover and bring to a boil. Once boiling, lower fire to a simmer and let it cook for 7 minutes.
4. With a handheld blender, puree mixture until smooth and creamy.
5. Stir in mushrooms and milk, cover, and simmer for another 8 minutes.
6. Serve and enjoy.

**Nutrition Info:**

- Info Per Servings 8.5g Carbs, 3.8g Protein, 1.0g Fat, 58.2 Calories

# Arugula Prawn Salad With Mayo Dressing

Servings: 4

Cooking Time: 15 Minutes

**Ingredients:**

- 4 cups baby arugula
- ½ cup garlic mayonnaise
- 3 tbsp olive oil
- 1 lb tiger prawns, peeled and deveined
- 1 tsp Dijon mustard
- Salt and chili pepper to season
- 2 tbsp lemon juice

**Directions:**

1. Add the mayonnaise, lemon juice and mustard in a small bowl. Mix until smooth and creamy. Heat 2 tbps of olive oil in a skillet over medium heat, add the prawns, season with salt, and chili pepper, and fry in the oil for 3 minutes on each side until prawns are pink. Set aside to a plate.
2. Place the arugula in a serving bowl and pour half of the dressing on the salad. Toss with 2 spoons until mixed, and add the remaining dressing. Divide salad into 4 plates and serve with prawns.

**Nutrition Info:**

- Info Per Servings 2g Carbs, 8g Protein, 20.3g Fat, 215 Calories

# Chicken Creamy Soup

Servings: 4

Cooking Time: 15 Minutes

**Ingredients:**

- 2 cups cooked and shredded chicken
- 3 tbsp butter, melted
- 4 cups chicken broth
- 4 tbsp chopped cilantro
- ⅓ cup buffalo sauce
- ½ cup cream cheese
- Salt and black pepper, to taste

**Directions:**

1. Blend the butter, buffalo sauce, and cream cheese, in a food processor, until smooth. Transfer to a pot, add the chicken broth and heat until hot but do not bring to a boil. Stir in chicken, salt, black pepper and cook until heated through. When ready, remove to soup bowls and serve garnished with cilantro.

**Nutrition Info:**

- Info Per Servings 5g Carbs, 26.5g Protein, 29.5g Fat, 406 Calories

# Caesar Salad With Chicken And Parmesan

Servings: 4

Cooking Time: 1 Hour And 30 Minutes

## Ingredients:

- 4 boneless, skinless chicken thighs
- ¼ cup lemon juice
- 2 garlic cloves, minced
- 4 tbsp olive oil
- ½ cup caesar salad dressing, sugar-free
- 12 bok choy leaves
- 3 Parmesan crisps
- Parmesan cheese, grated for garnishing

## Directions:

1. Combine the chicken, lemon juice, 2 tbsp of olive oil, and garlic in a Ziploc bag. Seal the bag, shake to combine, and refrigerate for 1 hour. Preheat the grill to medium heat and grill the chicken for about 4 minutes per side.
2. Cut the bok choy leaves lengthwise, and brush it with the remaining olive oil. Grill the bok choy for about 3 minutes. Place on a serving bowl. Top with the chicken and drizzle the caesar salad dressing over. Top with parmesan crisps and sprinkle the grated parmesan cheese over.

## Nutrition Info:

- Info Per Servings 5g Carbs, 33g Protein, 39g Fat, 529 Calories

## Sour Cream And Cucumbers

Servings: 8

Cooking Time: 0 Minutes

## Ingredients:

- ½ cup sour cream
- 3 tablespoons white vinegar
- 4 medium cucumbers, sliced thinly
- 1 small sweet onion, sliced thinly
- Salt and pepper to taste
- 3 tablespoons olive oil

## Directions:

1. In a bowl, whisk the sour cream and vinegar. Season with salt and pepper to taste. Whisk until well-combined.
2. Add in the cucumber and the rest of the ingredients.
3. Toss to coat.
4. Allow chilling before serving.

## Nutrition Info:

- Info Per Servings 4.8g Carbs, 0.9g Protein, 8.3g Fat, 96 Calories

## Strawberry Salad With Spinach, Cheese & Almonds

Servings: 2

Cooking Time: 20 Minutes

## Ingredients:

- 4 cups spinach
- 4 strawberries, sliced
- ½ cup flaked almonds
- 1 ½ cup grated hard goat cheese
- 4 tbsp raspberry vinaigrette
- Salt and black pepper, to taste

## Directions:

1. Preheat your oven to 400ºF. Arrange the grated goat cheese in two circles on two pieces of parchment paper. Place in the oven and bake for 10 minutes.
2. Find two same bowls, place them upside down, and carefully put the parchment paper on top to give the cheese a bowl-like shape. Let cool that way for 15 minutes. Divide spinach among the bowls stir in salt, pepper and drizzle with vinaigrette. Top with almonds and strawberries.

## Nutrition Info:

- Info Per Servings 5.3g Carbs, 33g Protein, 34.2g Fat, 445 Calories

# Homemade Cold Gazpacho Soup

Servings: 6

Cooking Time: 15 Minutes

**Ingredients:**

- 2 small green peppers, roasted
- 2 large red peppers, roasted
- 2 medium avocados, flesh scoped out
- 2 garlic cloves
- 2 spring onions, chopped
- 1 cucumber, chopped
- 1 cup olive oil
- 2 tbsp lemon juice
- 4 tomatoes, chopped
- 7 ounces goat cheese
- 1 small red onion, chopped
- 2 tbsp apple cider vinegar
- Salt to taste

**Directions:**

1. Place the peppers, tomatoes, avocados, red onion, garlic, lemon juice, olive oil, vinegar, and salt, in a food processor. Pulse until your desired consistency is reached. Taste and adjust the seasoning.
2. Transfer the mixture to a pot. Stir in cucumber and spring onions. Cover and chill in the fridge at least 2 hours. Divide the soup between 6 bowls. Serve very cold, generously topped with goat cheese and an extra drizzle of olive oil.

**Nutrition Info:**

- Info Per Servings 6.5g Carbs, 7.5g Protein, 45.8g Fat, 528 Calories

# Green Salad

Servings: 4

Cooking Time: 30 Minutes

**Ingredients:**

- 2 cups green beans, chopped
- 2 cups shredded spinach
- ½ cup parmesan cheese
- 3 cups basil leaves
- 3 cloves of garlic
- Salt to taste
- ¼ cup olive oil

**Directions:**

1. Heat a little olive oil in a skillet over medium heat and add the green beans and season with salt to taste. Sauté for 3 to 5 minutes.
2. Place the green beans in a bowl and add in the spinach.
3. In a food processor, combine half of the parmesan cheese, basil, and garlic. Add in the rest of the oil and season with salt and pepper to taste.
4. Pour into the green beans and toss to coat the ingredients.

**Nutrition Info:**

- Info Per Servings 6g Carbs, 5g Protein, 17g Fat, 196 Calories

# Mushroom Soup

Servings: 8

Cooking Time: 35 Minutes

**Ingredients:**

- 1-pound baby portobello mushrooms, chopped
- 2 tablespoons olive oil
- 1 carton reduced-sodium beef broth
- 2 cups heavy whipping cream
- 4 tablespoons butter
- 1/2 cup water

**Directions:**

1. In a Dutch oven, sauté mushrooms in oil and butter until tender.
2. Add the contents of seasoning packets, broth, and water. Bring to a boil.
3. Reduce heat; cover and simmer for 25 minutes.
4. Add cream and heat through.

**Nutrition Info:**

- Info Per Servings 3.6g Carbs, 8g Protein, 26g Fat, 280 Calories

# Power Green Soup

Servings: 6

Cooking Time: 30 Minutes

**Ingredients:**

- 1 broccoli head, chopped
- 1 cup spinach
- 1 onion, chopped
- 2 garlic cloves, minced
- ½ cup watercress
- 5 cups veggie stock
- 1 cup coconut milk
- 1 tsp salt
- 1 tbsp ghee
- 1 bay leaf
- Salt and black pepper, to taste

**Directions:**

1. Melt the ghee in a large pot over medium heat. Add onion and cook for 3 minutes. Add garlic and cook for another minute. Add broccoli and cook for an additional 5 minutes.
2. Pour the stock over and add the bay leaf. Close the lid, bring to a boil, and reduce the heat. Simmer for about 3 minutes.
3. In the end, add spinach and watercress, and cook for 3 more minutes. Stir in the coconut cream, salt and pepper. Discard the bay leaf, and blend the soup with a hand blender.

**Nutrition Info:**

- Info Per Servings 5.8g Carbs, 4.9g Protein, 37.6g Fat, 392 Calories

# Traditional Greek Salad

Servings: 4

Cooking Time: 10 Minutes

**Ingredients:**

- 5 tomatoes, chopped
- 1 large cucumber, chopped
- 1 green bell pepper, chopped
- 1 small red onion, chopped
- 16 kalamata olives, chopped
- 4 tbsp capers
- 1 cup feta cheese, chopped
- 1 tsp oregano, dried
- 4 tbsp olive oil
- Salt to taste

**Directions:**

1. Place tomatoes, bell pepper, cucumber, onion, feta cheese and olives in a bowl; mix to combine well. Season with salt. Combine capers, olive oil, and oregano, in a small bowl. Drizzle with the dressing to serve.

**Nutrition Info:**

- Info Per Servings 8g Carbs, 9.3g Protein, 28g Fat, 323 Calories

# Salmon Salad With Walnuts

Servings: 2

Cooking Time: 10 Minutes

**Ingredients:**

- 2 salmon fillets
- 2 tablespoons balsamic vinaigrette, divided
- 1/8 teaspoon pepper
- 2 cups mixed salad greens
- 1/4 cup walnuts
- 2 tablespoons crumbled cheese
- Salt and pepper to taste
- 3 tablespoons olive oil

**Directions:**

1. Brush the salmon with half of the balsamic vinaigrette and sprinkle with pepper.
2. Grill the salmon over medium heat for 5 minutes on each side.
3. Crumble the salmon and place in a mixing bowl. Add the rest of the ingredients and season with salt and pepper to taste.

**Nutrition Info:**

- Info Per Servings 8g Carbs, 5g Protein, 30g Fat, 313 Calories

# Caesar Salad With Smoked Salmon And Poached Eggs

Servings: 4

Cooking Time: 15 Minutes

**Ingredients:**

- 3 cups water
- 8 eggs
- 2 cups torn romaine lettuce
- ½ cup smoked salmon, chopped
- 6 slices bacon
- 2 tbsp Heinz low carb Caesar dressing

**Directions:**

1. Boil the water in a pot over medium heat for 5 minutes and bring to simmer. Crack each egg into a small bowl and gently slide into the water. Poach for 2 to 3 minutes, remove with a perforated spoon, transfer to a paper towel to dry, and plate. Poach the remaining 7 eggs.
2. Put the bacon in a skillet and fry over medium heat until browned and crispy, about 6 minutes, turning once. Remove, allow cooling, and chop in small pieces.
3. Toss the lettuce, smoked salmon, bacon, and caesar dressing in a salad bowl. Divide the salad into 4 plates, top with two eggs each, and serve immediately or chilled.

**Nutrition Info:**

- Info Per Servings 5g Carbs, 8g Protein, 21g Fat, 260 Calories

# Pork Burger Salad With Yellow Cheddar

Servings: 4

Cooking Time: 25 Minutes

**Ingredients:**

- 1 lb ground pork
- Salt and black pepper to season
- 1 tbsp olive oil
- 2 hearts romaine lettuce, torn into pieces
- 2 firm tomatoes, sliced
- ¼ red onion, sliced
- 3 oz yellow cheddar cheese, shredded

**Directions:**

1. Season the pork with salt and black pepper, mix and make medium-sized patties out of them.
2. Heat the oil in a skillet over medium heat and fry the patties on both sides for 10 minutes until browned and cook within. Transfer to a wire rack to drain oil. When cooled, cut into quarters.
3. Mix the lettuce, tomatoes, and red onion in a salad bowl, season with a little oil, salt, and pepper. Toss and add the pork on top.
4. Melt the cheese in the microwave for about 90 seconds. Drizzle the cheese over the salad and serve.

**Nutrition Info:**

- Info Per Servings 2g Carbs, 22g Protein, 23g Fat, 310 Calories

# Mediterranean Salad

Servings: 4

Cooking Time: 10 Minutes

**Ingredients:**

- 3 tomatoes, sliced
- 1 large avocado, sliced
- 8 kalamata olives
- ¼ lb buffalo mozzarella cheese, sliced
- 2 tbsp pesto sauce
- 2 tbsp olive oil

**Directions:**

1. Arrange the tomato slices on a serving platter and place the avocado slices in the middle. Arrange the olives around the avocado slices and drop pieces of mozzarella on the platter. Drizzle the pesto sauce all over, and drizzle olive oil as well.

**Nutrition Info:**

- Info Per Servings 4.3g Carbs, 9g Protein, 25g Fat, 290 Calories

# Corn And Bacon Chowder

Servings: 8

Cooking Time: 23 Minutes

## Ingredients:

- ½ cup bacon, fried and crumbled
- 1 package celery, onion, and bell pepper mix
- 2 cups full-fat milk
- ½ cup sharp cheddar cheese, grated
- 5 tablespoons butter
- Pepper and salt to taste
- 1 cup water

## Directions:

1. In a heavy-bottomed pot, melt butter.
2. Saute the bacon and celery for 3 minutes.
3. Turn fire on to medium. Add remaining ingredients and cook for 20 minutes until thick.
4. Serve and enjoy with a sprinkle of crumbled bacon.

## Nutrition Info:

- Info Per Servings 4.4g Carbs, 16.6g Protein, 13.6g Fat, 210.5 Calories

# Green Mackerel Salad

Servings: 2

Cooking Time: 25 Minutes

## Ingredients:

- 2 mackerel fillets
- 2 hard-boiled eggs, sliced
- 1 tbsp coconut oil
- 2 cups green beans
- 1 avocado, sliced
- 4 cups mixed salad greens
- 2 tbsp olive oil
- 2 tbsp lemon juice
- 1 tsp Dijon mustard
- Salt and black pepper, to taste

## Directions:

1. Fill a saucepan with water and add the green beans and salt. Cook over medium heat for about 3 minutes. Drain and set aside.
2. Melt the coconut oil in a pan over medium heat. Add the mackerel fillets and cook for about 4 minutes per side, or until opaque and crispy. Divide the green beans between two salad bowls. Top with mackerel, egg, and avocado slices.
3. In a bowl, whisk together the lemon juice, olive oil, mustard, salt, and pepper, and drizzle over the salad.

## Nutrition Info:

- Info Per Servings 7.6g Carbs, 27.3g Protein, 41.9g Fat, 525 Calories

# Sriracha Egg Salad With Mustard Dressing

Servings: 8

Cooking Time: 15 Minutes

## Ingredients:

- 10 eggs
- ¾ cup mayonnaise
- 1 tsp sriracha
- 1 tbsp mustard
- ½ cup scallions
- ½ stalk celery, minced
- ½ tsp fresh lemon juice
- ½ tsp sea salt
- ½ tsp black pepper, to taste
- 1 head romaine lettuce, torn into pieces

## Directions:

1. Add the eggs in a pan and cover with enough water and boil. Get them from the heat and allow to set for 10 minutes while covered. Chop the eggs and add to a salad bowl.
2. Stir in the remaining ingredients until everything is well combined. Refrigerate until ready to serve.

## Nutrition Info:

- Info Per Servings 7.7g Carbs, 7.4g Protein, 13g Fat, 174 Calories

# Creamy Cauliflower Soup

Servings: 4

Cooking Time: 20 Minutes

**Ingredients:**

- 1 cauliflower head, chopped
- ½ cup onions, chopped
- 4 cups chicken broth
- 1 tablespoon butter
- 1 cup heavy cream
- Pepper and salt to taste

**Directions:**

1. Place all ingredients in a pot on medium-high fire, except for the heavy cream.
2. Season with salt and pepper to taste.
3. Give a good stir to combine everything.
4. Cover and bring to a boil, and simmer for 15 minutes.
5. With an immersion blender, blend well until smooth and creamy.
6. Stir in heavy cream and continue simmering for another 5 minutes. Adjust seasoning if needed.
7. Serve and enjoy.

**Nutrition Info:**

- Info Per Servings 7.3g Carbs, 53.9g Protein, 30.8g Fat, 531 Calories

# Chicken Taco Soup

Servings: 6

Cooking Time: 45 Minutes

**Ingredients:**

- 1-pound boneless chicken breast
- 1 tbsp taco seasoning
- 3 medium tomato chopped
- 1 medium onion chopped
- 2 Tablespoons garlic minced
- 5 cups water
- Salt and Pepper to taste
- Sour cream or tortilla chips for topping (optional)

**Directions:**

1. Add all ingredients in a heavy-bottomed pot except for garnish if using.
2. Bring to a boil, lower fire to a simmer, cover and cook for 30 minutes.
3. Remove chicken and shred. Return to the pot. Adjust seasoning with pepper and salt to taste.
4. Serve and enjoy with topping.

**Nutrition Info:**

- Info Per Servings 5.0g Carbs, 15.0g Protein, 2.0g Fat, 98 Calories

# Shrimp With Avocado & Cauliflower Salad

Servings: 6

Cooking Time: 30 Minutes

**Ingredients:**

- 1 cauliflower head, florets only
- 1 pound medium shrimp
- ¼ cup + 1 tbsp olive oil
- 1 avocado, chopped
- 3 tbsp chopped dill
- ¼ cup lemon juice
- 2 tbsp lemon zest
- Salt and black pepper to taste

**Directions:**

1. Heat 1 tbsp olive oil in a skillet and cook the shrimp until opaque, about 8-10 minutes. Place the cauliflower florets in a microwave-safe bowl, and microwave for 5 minutes. Place the shrimp, cauliflower, and avocado in a large bowl.
2. Whisk together the remaining olive oil, lemon zest, juice, dill, and some salt and pepper, in another bowl. Pour the dressing over, toss to combine and serve immediately.

**Nutrition Info:**

- Info Per Servings 5g Carbs, 15g Protein, 17g Fat, 214 Calories

# Crunchy And Salty Cucumber

Servings: 4

Cooking Time: 0 Minutes

**Ingredients:**

- 2 Persian cucumbers, sliced thinly
- 1 medium radish, trimmed and sliced thinly
- Juice from 1 lemon
- ½ cup parmesan cheese, shredded
- A dash of flaky sea salt
- A dash of ground black pepper
- 5 tablespoons olive oil

**Directions:**

1. Place all vegetables in a bowl.
2. Stir in the lemon juice and parmesan cheese.
3. Season with salt and pepper to taste
4. Add olive oil or salad oil.
5. Toss to mix everything.

**Nutrition Info:**

- Info Per Servings 4g Carbs, 3.7g Protein, 20g Fat, 209 Calories

# Asparagus Niçoise Salad

Servings: 4

Cooking Time: 0 Minutes

**Ingredients:**

- 1-pound fresh asparagus, trimmed and blanched
- 2 ½ ounces white tuna in oil
- ½ cup pitted Greek olives, halved
- ½ cup zesty Italian salad dressing
- Salt and pepper to taste
- 3 tablespoons olive oil

**Directions:**

1. Place all ingredients in a bowl.
2. Toss to mix all ingredients.
3. Serve.

**Nutrition Info:**

- Info Per Servings 10g Carbs, 8g Protein, 20g Fat,

239 Calories

# Fruit Salad With Poppy Seeds

Servings: 5

Cooking Time: 25 Mins

**Ingredients:**

- 1 tablespoon poppy seeds
- 1 head romaine lettuce, torn into bite-size pieces
- 4 ounces shredded Swiss cheese
- 1 avocado- peeled, cored and diced
- 2 teaspoons diced onion
- 1/2 cup lemon juice
- 1/2 cup stevia
- 1/2 teaspoon salt
- 2/3 cup olive oil
- 1 teaspoon Dijon style prepared mustard

**Directions:**

1. Combine stevia, lemon juice, onion, mustard, and salt in a blender. Process until well blended.
2. Add oil until mixture is thick and smooth. Add poppy seeds, stir just a few seconds or more to mix.
3. In a large serving bowl, toss together the remaining ingredients.
4. Pour dressing over salad just before serving, and toss to coat.

**Nutrition Info:**

- Info Per Servings 6g Carbs, 4.9g Protein, 20.6g Fat, 277 Calories

# Pork, Beef &
# Lamb Recipes

# Pork, Beef & Lamb Recipes

## Mushroom Beef Stew

Servings: 5

Cooking Time: 1h 30mins

**Ingredients:**

- 2 pounds beef chuck roast, cut into 1/2-inch thick strips
- 1/2 medium onion, sliced or diced
- 8 ounces sliced mushrooms
- 2 cups beef broth, divided
- Salt and pepper to taste
- 1 tablespoon butter
- 2 cloves garlic, minced
- 1 tablespoon fresh chopped chives
- 1 tablespoon olive oil

**Directions:**

1. Heat olive oil in a large skillet over high heat. Stir in beef with salt and pepper; cook, stirring constantly, for 6-7 minutes. Remove beef from the pan and set aside.
2. Add butter, mushrooms and onions into the pan; cook and stir over medium heat.
3. Add garlic and stir for 30 seconds. Stir in 1 cup. broth and simmer 3-4 minutes.
4. Return beef to the pan. Stir in remaining broth and chives; bring to a simmer and cook on low heat for about 1 hour, covered, stirring every 20 minutes.
5. Season with salt and pepper to taste. Serve.

**Nutrition Info:**

- Info Per Servings 4.1g Carbs, 15.8g Protein, 24.5g Fat, 307 Calories

## Pork Osso Bucco

Servings: 6

Cooking Time: 1 Hour 55 Minutes

**Ingredients:**

- 4 tbsp butter, softened
- 6 pork shanks
- 2 tbsp olive oil
- 3 cloves garlic, minced
- 1 cup diced tomatoes
- Salt and black pepper to taste
- ½ cup chopped onions
- ½ cup chopped celery
- ½ cup chopped carrots
- 2 cups Cabernet Sauvignon
- 5 cups beef broth
- ½ cup chopped parsley + extra to garnish
- 2 tsp lemon zest

**Directions:**

1. Melt the butter in a large saucepan over medium heat. Season the pork with salt and pepper and brown it for 12 minutes; remove to a plate.
2. In the same pan, sauté 2 cloves of garlic and onions in the oil, for 3 minutes then return the pork shanks. Stir in the Cabernet, carrots, celery, tomatoes, and beef broth with a season of salt and pepper. Cover the pan and let it simmer on low heat for 1 ½ hours basting the pork every 15 minutes with the sauce.
3. In a bowl, mix the remaining garlic, parsley, and lemon zest to make a gremolata, and stir the mixture into the sauce when it is ready. Turn the heat off and dish the Osso Bucco. Garnish with parsley and serve with a creamy turnip mash.

**Nutrition Info:**

- Info Per Servings 6.1g Carbs, 34g Protein, 40g Fat, 590 Calories

# Baked Pork Meatballs In Pasta Sauce

Servings: 6

Cooking Time: 45 Minutes

**Ingredients:**

- 2 lb ground pork
- 1 tbsp olive oil
- 1 cup pork rinds, crushed
- 3 cloves garlic, minced
- ½ cup coconut milk
- 2 eggs, beaten
- ½ cup grated Parmesan cheese
- ½ cup grated asiago cheese
- Salt and black pepper to taste
- ¼ cup chopped parsley
- 2 jars sugar-free marinara sauce
- ½ tsp Italian seasoning
- 1 cup Italian blend kinds of cheeses
- Chopped basil to garnish
- Cooking spray

**Directions:**

1. Preheat the oven to 400°F, line a cast iron pan with foil and oil it with cooking spray. Set aside.
2. Combine the coconut milk and pork rinds in a bowl. Mix in the ground pork, garlic, Asiago cheese, Parmesan cheese, eggs, salt, and pepper, just until combined. Form balls of the mixture and place them in the prepared pan. Bake in the oven for 20 minutes at a reduced temperature of 370°F.
3. Transfer the meatballs to a plate. Remove the foil and pour in half of the marinara sauce. Place the meatballs back in the pan and pour the remaining marinara sauce all over them. Sprinkle all over with the Italian blend cheeses, drizzle the olive oil on them, and then sprinkle with Italian seasoning.
4. Cover the pan with foil and put it back in the oven to bake for 10 minutes. After, remove the foil, and continue cooking for 5 minutes. Once ready, take out the pan and garnish with basil. Serve on a bed of squash spaghetti.

**Nutrition Info:**

- Info Per Servings 4.1g Carbs, 46.2g Protein, 46.8g Fat, 590 Calories

# Pork Burgers With Caramelized Onion Rings

Servings: 6

Cooking Time: 20 Minutes

**Ingredients:**

- 2 lb ground pork
- Pink salt and chili pepper to taste
- 3 tbsp olive oil
- 1 tbsp butter
- 1 white onion, sliced into rings
- 1 tbsp balsamic vinegar
- 3 drops liquid stevia
- 6 low carb burger buns, halved
- 2 firm tomatoes, sliced into rings

**Directions:**

1. Combine the pork, salt and chili pepper in a bowl and mold out 6 patties.
2. Heat the olive oil in a skillet over medium heat and fry the patties for 4 to 5 minutes on each side until golden brown on the outside. Remove onto a plate and sit for 3 minutes.
3. Meanwhile, melt butter in a skillet over medium heat, sauté the onions for 2 minutes to be soft, and stir in the balsamic vinegar and liquid stevia.
4. Cook for 30 seconds stirring once or twice until caramelized. In each bun, place a patty, top with some onion rings and 2 tomato rings. Serve the burgers with cheddar cheese dip.

**Nutrition Info:**

- Info Per Servings 7.6g Carbs, 26g Protein, 32g Fat, 445 Calories

# Ground Beef And Cabbage Stir Fry

Servings: 5

Cooking Time:20 Minutes

**Ingredients:**

- 1 onion, chopped
- 3 cloves of garlic, minced
- 1 ½ pounds ground beef
- 1 tablespoon grated ginger
- ½ head cabbage, chopped
- 2 tablespoons oil
- Salt and pepper to taste
- 1 teaspoon chili flakes (optional)

**Directions:**

1. In a skillet, heat oil over medium flame.
2. Sauté the onion and garlic until fragrant.
3. Stir in the ground beef and season with salt and pepper to taste. Cook and crumble for 10 minutes.
4. Add grated ginger, chopped cabbage, and chili flakes. Cover and cook for 5 minutes.
5. Stir and continue cooking for another 3 minutes or until cabbage is translucent and wilted.
6. Serve and enjoy.

**Nutrition Info:**

- Info Per Servings 6.3g Carbs, 30.6g Protein, 23.7g Fat, 385 Calories

# Chuck Roast Beef

Servings: 6

Cooking Time: 3 Hours 15 Minutes

**Ingredients:**

- 2 pounds beef chuck roast, cubed
- 2 tbsp olive oil
- 14.5 ounces canned diced tomatoes
- 2 carrots, chopped
- Salt and black pepper, to taste
- ½ pound mushrooms, sliced
- 2 celery stalks, chopped
- 2 yellow onions, chopped

- 1 cup beef stock
- 1 tbsp fresh thyme, chopped
- ½ tsp dry mustard
- 3 tbsp almond flour
- 1 cup water

**Directions:**

1. Set an ovenproof pot over medium heat, warm olive oil and brown the beef on each side for a few minutes. Stir in the tomatoes, onions, salt, pepper, mustard, carrots, mushrooms, celery, and stock.
2. In a bowl, combine the water with flour. Place this to the pot, stir then set in the oven, and bake for 3 hours at 325ºF stirring at intervals of 30 minutes. Scatter the fresh thyme over and serve warm.

**Nutrition Info:**

- Info Per Servings 7g Carbs, 28g Protein, 18g Fat, 325 Calories

# Beef Skewers With Ranch Dressing

Servings: 4

Cooking Time: 25 Minutes

**Ingredients:**

- 1 lb sirloin steak, boneless, cubed
- ¼ cup ranch dressing, divided
- Chopped scallions to garnish

**Directions:**

1. Preheat the grill on medium heat to 400ºF and thread the beef cubes on the skewers, about 4 to 5 cubes per skewer. Brush half of the ranch dressing on the skewers (all around) and place them on the grill grate to cook for 6 minutes. Turn the skewers once and cook further for 6 minutes.
2. Brush the remaining ranch dressing on the meat and cook them for 1 more minute on each side. Plate, garnish with the scallions, and serve with a mixed veggie salad, and extra ranch dressing.

**Nutrition Info:**

- Info Per Servings 3g Carbs, 21g Protein, 14g Fat, 230 Calories

# Hot Pork With Dill Pickles

Servings: 4

Cooking Time: 20 Minutes

**Ingredients:**

- ¼ cup lime juice
- 4 pork chops
- 1 tbsp coconut oil, melted
- 2 garlic cloves, minced
- 1 tbsp chili powder
- 1 tsp ground cinnamon
- 2 tsp cumin
- Salt and black pepper, to taste
- ½ tsp hot pepper sauce
- 4 dill pickles, cut into spears and squeezed

**Directions:**

1. Using a bowl, combine the lime juice with oil, cumin, salt, hot pepper sauce, pepper, cinnamon, garlic, and chili powder. Place in the pork chops, toss to coat, and refrigerate for 4 hours.
2. Arrange the pork on a preheated grill over medium heat, cook for 7 minutes, turn, add in the dill pickles, and cook for another 7 minutes. Split among serving plates and enjoy.

**Nutrition Info:**

- Info Per Servings 2.3g Carbs, 36g Protein, 18g Fat, 315 Calories

# Zucchini Boats With Beef And Pimiento Rojo

Servings: 4

Cooking Time: 30 Minutes

**Ingredients:**

- 4 zucchinis
- 2 tbsp olive oil
- 1 ½ lb ground beef
- 1 medium red onion, chopped
- 2 tbsp chopped pimiento
- Pink salt and black pepper to taste
- 1 cup grated yellow cheddar cheese

**Directions:**

1. Preheat oven to 350ºF.
2. Lay the zucchinis on a flat surface, trim off the ends and cut in half lengthwise. Scoop out pulp from each half with a spoon to make shells. Chop the pulp.
3. Heat oil in a skillet; add the ground beef, red onion, pimiento, and zucchini pulp, and season with salt and black pepper. Cook for 6 minutes while stirring to break up lumps until beef is no longer pink. Turn the heat off. Spoon the beef into the boats and sprinkle with cheddar cheese.
4. Place on a greased baking sheet and cook to melt the cheese for 15 minutes until zucchini boats are tender. Take out, cool for 2 minutes, and serve warm with a mixed green salad.

**Nutrition Info:**

- Info Per Servings 7g Carbs, 18g Protein, 24g Fat, 335 Calories

# Cherry-balsamic Sauced Beef

Servings: 4

Cooking Time: 40 Minutes

**Ingredients:**

- 2-lbs London broil beef, sliced into 2-inch cubes
- 1/3 cup balsamic vinegar
- ½ cup dried cherries
- ½ teaspoon pepper
- 1 teaspoon salt
- 1 tablespoon canola oil
- ½ cup water

**Directions:**

1. Add all ingredients in a pot on high fire and bring to a boil.
2. Once boiling, lower fire to a simmer and cook for 35 minutes.
3. Adjust seasoning to taste.
4. Serve and enjoy.

**Nutrition Info:**

- Info Per Servings 4.6g Carbs, 82.2g Protein, 17.2g Fat, 525 Calories

# Adobo Beef Fajitas

Servings: 4

Cooking Time: 35 Minutes

## Ingredients:

- 2 lb skirt steak, cut in halves
- 2 tbsp Adobo seasoning
- Pink salt to taste
- 2 tbsp olive oil
- 2 large white onion, chopped
- 1 cup sliced mixed bell peppers, chopped
- 12 low carb tortillas

## Directions:

1. Season the steak with adobo and marinate in the fridge for one hour.
2. Preheat grill to 425ºF and cook steak for 6 minutes on each side, flipping once until lightly browned. Remove from heat and wrap in foil and let sit for 10 minutes. This allows the meat to cook in its heat for a few more minutes before slicing.
3. Heat the olive oil in a skillet over medium heat and sauté the onion and bell peppers for 5 minutes or until soft. Cut steak against the grain into strips and share on the tortillas. Top with the veggies and serve with guacamole.

## Nutrition Info:

- Info Per Servings 5g Carbs, 18g Protein, 25g Fat, 348 Calories

# Beef And Cabbage With Spice Packet

Servings: 5

Cooking Time: 1h 20mins

## Ingredients:

- 3 pounds corned beef brisket with spice packet
- 1 large head cabbage, cut into small wedges
- 1 cup diced onion
- 3 cups water
- 2 cups beef broth

## Directions:

1. Place corned beef in large pot and cover with water. Add the spice packet to the corned beef.
2. Cover the pot and bring to a boil, simmering for 50 minutes.
3. Add the cabbage and onion, cook until the vegetables are almost tender.
4. Remove beef and cool for 15 minutes.
5. Transfer vegetables into a bowl and cover. Add as much broth as you want. Slice meat across the grain. Serve and enjoy.

## Nutrition Info:

- Info Per Servings 11g Carbs, 21g Protein, 23.7g Fat, 341 Calories

# Jalapeno Beef Pot Roasted

Servings: 4

Cooking Time: 1 Hour 25 Minutes

## Ingredients:

- 3½ pounds beef roast
- 4 ounces mushrooms, sliced
- 12 ounces beef stock
- 1 ounce onion soup mix
- ½ cup Italian dressing
- 2 jalapeños, shredded

## Directions:

1. Using a bowl, combine the stock with the Italian dressing and onion soup mixture. Place the beef roast in a pan, stir in the stock mixture, mushrooms, and jalapeños; cover with aluminum foil.
2. Set in the oven at 300ºF, and bake for 1 hour. Take out the foil and continue baking for 15 minutes. Allow the roast to cool, slice, and serve alongside a topping of the gravy.

## Nutrition Info:

- Info Per Servings 3.2g Carbs, 87g Protein, 46g Fat, 745 Calories

## Dr. Pepper Pulled Pork

Servings: 9

Cooking Time: 45 Minutes

**Ingredients:**

- 3 pounds pork loin roast, chopped into 8 equal pieces
- 1 packet pork rub seasoning
- 1 12-ounce can Dr. Pepper
- ½ cup commercial BBQ sauce
- 1 bay leaf
- 1 tsp oil
- 2 tbsp water

**Directions:**

1. Place a heavy-bottomed pot on medium-high fire and heat for 2 minutes. Add oil and swirl to coat the bottom and sides of pot and heat for a minute.
2. Brown roast for 4 minutes per side.
3. Add remaining ingredients.
4. Cover and simmer for 30 minutes or until pork is fork-tender. Stir the bottom of the pot every now and then. Turn off the fire.
5. With two forks, shred pork.
6. Turn on fire to high and boil uncovered until sauce is rendered, around 5 minutes.
7. Serve and enjoy.

**Nutrition Info:**

- Info Per Servings 4.6g Carbs, 40.9g Protein, 13.4g Fat, 310 Calories

## Beef Cauliflower Curry

Servings: 6

Cooking Time: 26 Minutes

**Ingredients:**

- 1 tbsp olive oil
- 1 ½ lb ground beef
- 1 tbsp ginger-garlic paste
- 1 tsp garam masala
- 1 can whole tomatoes
- 1 head cauliflower, cut into florets
- Pink salt and chili pepper to taste

- ¼ cup water

**Directions:**

1. Heat oil in a saucepan over medium heat, add the beef, ginger-garlic paste and season with garam masala. Cook for 5 minutes while breaking any lumps.
2. Stir in the tomatoes and cauliflower, season with salt and chili pepper, and cook covered for 6 minutes. Add the water and bring to a boil over medium heat for 10 minutes or until the water has reduced by half. Adjust taste with salt.
3. Spoon the curry into serving bowls and serve with shirataki rice.

**Nutrition Info:**

- Info Per Servings 2g Carbs, 22g Protein, 33g Fat, 374 Calories

## Classic Italian Bolognese Sauce

Servings: 5

Cooking Time: 35 Minutes

**Ingredients:**

- 1 pound ground beef
- 2 garlic cloves
- 1 onion, chopped
- 1 tsp oregano
- 1 tsp sage
- 1 tsp marjoram
- 1 tsp rosemary
- 7 oz canned chopped tomatoes
- 1 tbsp olive oil

**Directions:**

1. Heat olive oil in a saucepan. Add onion and garlic and cook for 3 minutes. Add beef and cook until browned, about 4-5 minutes. Stir in the herbs and tomatoes. Cook for 15 minutes. Serve with zoodles.

**Nutrition Info:**

- Info Per Servings 5.9g Carbs, 26g Protein, 20g Fat, 318 Calories

# Cranberry Gravy Brisket

Servings: 7

Cooking Time: 25 Minutes

**Ingredients:**

- 1 tablespoon prepared mustard
- ½ cup chopped onion
- 1 can tomato sauce
- ½ cup cranberries, pitted
- 1 fresh beef brisket
- 5 tablespoons olive oil
- ½ teaspoon salt
- ¼ teaspoon pepper

**Directions:**

1. Add all ingredients in a pot on high fire and bring to a boil.
2. Once boiling, lower fire to a simmer and cook for 25 minutes.
3. Adjust seasoning to taste.
4. Serve and enjoy.

**Nutrition Info:**

- Info Per Servings 9.7g Carbs, 24.9g Protein, 24.4g Fat, 364 Calories

# Italian Sausage Stew

Servings: 6

Cooking Time: 35 Minutes

**Ingredients:**

- 1 pound Italian sausage, sliced
- 1 red bell pepper, seeded and chopped
- 2 onions, chopped
- Salt and black pepper, to taste
- 1 cup fresh parsley, chopped
- 6 green onions, chopped
- ¼ cup avocado oil
- 1 cup beef stock
- 4 garlic cloves
- 24 ounces canned diced tomatoes
- 16 ounces okra, trimmed and sliced
- 6 ounces tomato sauce
- 2 tbsp coconut aminos
- 1 tbsp hot sauce

**Directions:**

1. Set a pot over medium-high heat and warm oil, place in the sausages, and cook for 2 minutes. Stir in the onion, green onions, garlic, pepper, bell pepper, and salt, and cook for 5 minutes.
2. Add in the hot sauce, stock, tomatoes, coconut aminos, okra, and tomato sauce, bring to a simmer and cook for 15 minutes. Adjust the seasoning with salt and pepper. Share into serving bowls and sprinkle with fresh parsley to serve.

**Nutrition Info:**

- Info Per Servings 7g Carbs, 16g Protein, 25g Fat, 314 Calories

# White Wine Lamb Chops

Servings: 6

Cooking Time: 1 Hour And 25 Minutes

**Ingredients:**

- 6 lamb chops
- 1 tbsp sage
- 1 tsp thyme
- 1 onion, sliced
- 3 garlic cloves, minced
- 2 tbsp olive oil
- ½ cup white wine
- Salt and black pepper, to taste

**Directions:**

1. Heat the olive oil in a pan. Add onion and garlic and cook for 3 minutes, until soft. Rub the sage and thyme over the lamb chops. Cook the lamb for about 3 minutes per side. Set aside.
2. Pour the white wine and 1 cup of water into the pan, bring the mixture to a boil. Cook until the liquid is reduced by half. Add the chops in the pan, reduce the heat, and let simmer for 1 hour.

**Nutrition Info:**

- Info Per Servings 4.3g Carbs, 16g Protein, 30g Fat, 397 Calories

# New York Strip Steak With Mushroom Sauce

Servings: 2

Cooking Time: 20 Minutes

**Ingredients:**

- 2 New York Strip steaks, trimmed from fat
- 3 cloves of garlic, minced
- 2 ounces shiitake mushrooms, sliced
- 2 ounces button mushrooms, sliced
- ¼ teaspoon thyme
- ¼ cup water
- ½ tsp salt
- 1 tsp pepper
- 5 tablespoons olive oil

**Directions:**

1. Heat the grill to 350F.
2. Position the grill rack 6 inches from the heat source.
3. Grill the steak for 10 minutes on each side or until slightly pink on the inside.
4. Meanwhile, prepare the sauce. In a small nonstick pan, water sauté the garlic, mushrooms, salt, pepper, and thyme for a minute. Pour in the broth and bring to a boil. Allow the sauce to simmer until the liquid is reduced.
5. Top the steaks with the mushroom sauce. Drizzle with olive oil.
6. Serve warm.

**Nutrition Info:**

- Info Per Servings 4.0g Carbs, 47.0g Protein, 36.0g Fat, 528 Calories

# Pork Casserole

Servings: 4

Cooking Time: 38 Minutes

**Ingredients:**

- 1 lb ground pork
- 1 large yellow squash, thinly sliced
- Salt and black pepper to taste
- 1 clove garlic, minced
- 4 green onions, chopped
- 1 cup chopped cremini mushrooms
- 1 can diced tomatoes
- ½ cup pork rinds, crushed
- ¼ cup chopped parsley
- 1 cup cottage cheese
- 1 cup Mexican cheese blend
- 3 tbsp olive oil
- ⅓ cup water

**Directions:**

1. Preheat the oven to 370°F.
2. Heat the olive oil in a skillet over medium heat, add the pork, season it with salt and pepper, and cook for 3 minutes or until no longer pink. Stir occasionally while breaking any lumps apart.
3. Add the garlic, half of the green onions, mushrooms, and 2 tablespoons of pork rinds. Continue cooking for 3 minutes. Stir in the tomatoes, half of the parsley, and water. Cook further for 3 minutes, and then turn the heat off.
4. Mix the remaining parsley, cottage cheese, and Mexican cheese blend. Set aside. Sprinkle the bottom of a baking dish with 3 tablespoons of pork rinds; top with half of the squash and a season of salt, 2/3 of the pork mixture, and the cheese mixture. Repeat the layering process a second time to exhaust the ingredients.
5. Cover the baking dish with foil and put in the oven to bake for 20 minutes. After, remove the foil and brown the top of the casserole with the broiler side of the oven for 2 minutes. Remove the dish when ready and serve the casserole warm.

**Nutrition Info:**

- Info Per Servings 2.7g Carbs, 36.5g Protein, 29g Fat, 495 Calories

# Paprika Pork Chops

Servings: 4

Cooking Time: 25 Minutes

**Ingredients:**

- 4 pork chops
- Salt and black pepper, to taste
- 3 tbsp paprika
- ¾ cup cumin powder
- 1 tsp chili powder

**Directions:**

1. Using a bowl, combine the paprika with pepper, cumin, salt, and chili. Place in the pork chops and rub them well. Heat a grill over medium temperature, add in the pork chops, cook for 5 minutes, flip, and cook for 5 minutes. Serve with steamed veggies.

**Nutrition Info:**

- Info Per Servings 4g Carbs, 41.8g Protein, 18.5g Fat, 349 Calories

# Creamy Pork Chops

Servings: 3

Cooking Time: 50 Minutes

**Ingredients:**

- 8 ounces mushrooms, sliced
- 1 tsp garlic powder
- 1 onion, peeled and chopped
- 1 cup heavy cream
- 3 pork chops, boneless
- 1 tsp ground nutmeg
- ¼ cup coconut oil

**Directions:**

1. Set a pan over medium heat and warm the oil, add in the onions and mushrooms, and cook for 4 minutes. Stir in the pork chops, season with garlic powder, and nutmeg, and sear until browned.
2. Put the pan in the oven at 350ºF, and bake for 30 minutes. Remove pork chops to bowls and main-

tain warm. Place the pan over medium heat, pour in the heavy cream and vinegar over the mushrooms mixture, and cook for 5 minutes; remove from heat. Sprinkle sauce over pork chops and enjoy.

**Nutrition Info:**

- Info Per Servings 6.8g Carbs, 42g Protein, 40g Fat, 612 Calories

# Beef And Feta Salad

Servings: 4

Cooking Time: 35 Minutes

**Ingredients:**

- 3 tbsp olive oil
- ½ pound beef rump steak, cut into strips
- Salt and ground black pepper, to taste
- 1 tsp cumin
- A pinch of dried thyme
- 2 garlic cloves, minced
- 4 ounces feta cheese, crumbled
- ½ cup pecans, toasted
- 2 cups spinach
- 1½ tbsp lemon juice
- ¼ cup fresh mint, chopped

**Directions:**

1. Season the beef with salt, 1 tbsp of olive oil, garlic, thyme, black pepper, and cumin. Place on preheated grill over medium-high heat, and cook for 10 minutes, flip once. Sprinkle the pecans on a lined baking sheet, place in the oven at 350ºF, and toast for 10 minutes.
2. Remove the grilled beef to a cutting board, leave to cool, and slice into strips.
3. In a salad bowl, combine the spinach with pepper, mint, remaining olive oil, salt, lemon juice, feta cheese, and pecans, and toss well to coat. Top with the beef slices and enjoy.

**Nutrition Info:**

- Info Per Servings 3.5g Carbs, 17g Protein, 43g Fat, 434 Calories

# Habanero And Beef Balls

Servings: 6

Cooking Time: 45 Minutes

## Ingredients:

- 3 garlic cloves, minced
- 1 pound ground beef
- 1 small onion, chopped
- 2 habanero peppers, chopped
- 1 tsp dried thyme
- 2 tsp cilantro
- ½ tsp allspice
- 2 tsp cumin
- A pinch of ground cloves
- Salt and black pepper, to taste
- 2 tbsp butter
- 3 tbsp butter, melted
- 6 ounces cream cheese
- 1 tsp turmeric
- ¼ tsp stevia
- ½ tsp baking powder
- 1½ cups flax meal
- ½ cup coconut flour

## Directions:

1. In a blender, mix onion with garlic, habaneros, and ½ cup water. Set a pan over medium heat, add in 2 tbsp butter and cook the beef for 3 minutes. Stir in the onion mixture, and cook for 2 minutes.
2. Stir in cilantro, cloves, salt, cumin, ½ teaspoon turmeric, thyme, allspice, and pepper, and cook for 3 minutes. In a bowl, combine the remaining turmeric, with coconut flour, stevia, flax meal, and baking powder. In a separate bowl, combine the 3 tbsp butter with the cream cheese.
3. Combine the 2 mixtures to obtain a dough. Form 12 balls from this mixture, set them on a parchment paper, and roll each into a circle. Split the beef mix on one-half of the dough circles, cover with the other half, seal edges, and lay on a lined sheet. Bake for 25 minutes in the oven at 350°F.

## Nutrition Info:

- Info Per Servings 8.3g Carbs, 27g Protein, 31g Fat, 455 Calories

# Mustard-lemon Beef

Servings: 4

Cooking Time: 25 Minutes

## Ingredients:

- 2 tbsp olive oil
- 1 tbsp fresh rosemary, chopped
- 2 garlic cloves, minced
- 1½ pounds beef rump steak, thinly sliced
- Salt and black pepper, to taste
- 1 shallot, chopped
- ½ cup heavy cream
- ½ cup beef stock
- 1 tbsp mustard
- 2 tsp Worcestershire sauce
- 2 tsp lemon juice
- 1 tsp erythritol
- 2 tbsp butter
- A sprig of rosemary
- A sprig of thyme

## Directions:

1. Using a bowl, combine 1 tbsp of oil with pepper, garlic, rosemary, and salt. Toss in the beef to coat, and set aside for some minutes. Heat a pan with the rest of the oil over medium-high heat, place in the beef steak, cook for 6 minutes, flipping halfway through; set aside and keep warm.
2. Set the pan to medium heat, stir in the shallot, and cook for 3 minutes; stir in the stock, Worcestershire sauce, erythritol, thyme, cream, mustard, and rosemary, and cook for 8 minutes.
3. Stir in the butter, lemon juice, pepper, and salt. Get rid of the rosemary and thyme, and remove from heat. Arrange the beef slices on serving plates, sprinkle over the sauce, and enjoy.

## Nutrition Info:

- Info Per Servings 5g Carbs, 32g Protein, 30g Fat, 435 Calories

# Poultry Recipes

## Chicken Paella With Chorizo

Servings: 6

Cooking Time: 63 Minutes

**Ingredients:**

- 18 chicken drumsticks
- 12 oz chorizo, chopped
- 1 white onion, chopped
- 4 oz jarred piquillo peppers, finely diced
- 2 tbsp olive oil
- ½ cup chopped parsley
- 1 tsp smoked paprika
- 2 tbsp tomato puree
- ½ cup white wine
- 1 cup chicken broth
- 2 cups cauli rice
- 1 cup chopped green beans
- 1 lemon, cut in wedges
- Salt and pepper, to taste

**Directions:**

1. Preheat the oven to 350°F.
2. Heat the olive oil in a cast iron pan over medium heat, meanwhile season the chicken with salt and pepper, and fry in the hot oil on both sides for 10 minutes to lightly brown. After, remove onto a plate with a perforated spoon.
3. Then, add the chorizo and onion to the hot oil, and sauté for 4 minutes. Include the tomato puree, piquillo peppers, and paprika, and let simmer for 2 minutes. Add the broth, and bring the ingredients to boil for 6 minutes until slightly reduced.
4. Stir in the cauli rice, white wine, green beans, half of the parsley, and lay the chicken on top. Transfer the pan to the oven and continue cooking for 20-25 minutes. Let the paella sit to cool for 10 minutes before serving garnished with the remaining parsley and lemon wedges.

**Nutrition Info:**

- Info Per Servings 3g Carbs, 22g Protein, 28g Fat, 440 Calories

## Chicken Wings With Thyme Chutney

Servings: 4

Cooking Time: 45 Minutes

**Ingredients:**

- 12 chicken wings, cut in half
- 1 tbsp turmeric
- 1 tbsp cumin
- 3 tbsp fresh ginger, grated
- 1 tbsp cilantro, chopped
- 2 tbsp paprika
- Salt and ground black pepper, to taste
- 3 tbsp olive oil
- Juice of ½ lime
- 1 cup thyme leaves
- ¾ cup cilantro, chopped
- 1 tbsp water
- 1 jalapeño pepper

**Directions:**

1. Using a bowl, stir together 1 tbsp ginger, cumin, paprika, salt, 2 tbsp olive oil, pepper, turmeric, and cilantro. Place in the chicken wings pieces, toss to coat, and refrigerate for 20 minutes. Heat the grill, place in the marinated wings, cook for 25 minutes, turning from time to time, remove and set to a bowl.
2. Using a blender, combine thyme, remaining ginger, salt, jalapeno pepper, black pepper, lime juice, cilantro, remaining olive oil, and water, and blend well. Set the chicken wings on serving plate and top with the sauce.

**Nutrition Info:**

- Info Per Servings 3.5g Carbs, 22g Protein, 15g Fat, 243 Calories

# Chicken In Creamy Mushroom Sauce

Servings: 4

Cooking Time: 36 Minutes

**Ingredients:**

- 1 tbsp ghee
- 4 chicken breasts, cut into chunks
- Salt and black pepper to taste
- 1 packet white onion soup mix
- 2 cups chicken broth
- 15 baby bella mushrooms, sliced
- 1 cup heavy cream
- 1 small bunch parsley, chopped

**Directions:**

1. Melt ghee in a saucepan over medium heat, season the chicken with salt and black pepper, and brown on all sides for 6 minutes in total. Put in a plate.
2. In a bowl, stir the onion soup mix with chicken broth and add to the saucepan. Simmer for 3 minutes and add the mushrooms and chicken. Cover and simmer for another 20 minutes.
3. Stir in heavy cream and parsley, cook on low heat for 3 minutes, and season with salt and pepper.
4. Ladle the chicken with creamy sauce and mushrooms over beds of cauli mash. Garnish with parsley.

**Nutrition Info:**

- Info Per Servings 2g Carbs, 22g Protein, 38.2g Fat, 448 Calories

## Chicken Pesto

Servings: 8

Cooking Time: 35 Minutes

**Ingredients:**

- 5 cloves of garlic
- 4 skinless, boneless chicken breast halves, cut into thin strips
- 3 tbsp grated Parmesan cheese
- ¼ cup pesto
- 1 ¼ cups heavy cream
- 10 tbsps olive oil
- Pepper to taste
- 1/8 tsp salt

**Directions:**

1. On medium fire, place a large saucepan and heat olive oil.
2. Add garlic and chicken, sauté for 7 minutes, or until chicken strips are nearly cooked.
3. Lower fire and add Parmesan cheese, pesto, cream, pepper, and salt.
4. Continue cooking for 5-10 minutes more or until chicken is fully cooked. Stir frequently.
5. Once penne is cooked, drain well and pour into a large saucepan, toss to coat, and serve.

**Nutrition Info:**

- Info Per Servings 3g Carbs, 30.0g Protein, 22.0g Fat, 330 Calories

## Oven-baked Skillet Lemon Chicken

Servings: 4

Cooking Time: 60 Minutes

**Ingredients:**

- 6 small chicken thighs
- 1 medium onion
- 1 lemon
- ¼ cup lemon juice, freshly squeezed
- Salt and pepper to taste

**Directions:**

1. Place all ingredients in a Ziploc bag and allow to marinate for at least 6 hours in the fridge.
2. Preheat the oven to 350F.
3. Place the chicken–sauce and all–into a skillet.
4. Put the skillet in the oven and bake for 1 hour or until the chicken is tender.

**Nutrition Info:**

- Info Per Servings 6.2g Carbs, 48.2g Protein, 42.4g Fat, 610 Calories

# Easy Chicken Meatloaf

Servings: 8

Cooking Time: 50 Minutes

## Ingredients:

- 1 cup sugar-free marinara sauce
- 2 lb ground chicken
- 2 tbsp fresh parsley, chopped
- 3 garlic cloves, minced
- 2 tsp onion powder
- 2 tsp Italian seasoning
- Salt and ground black pepper, to taste
- For the filling
- ½ cup ricotta cheese
- 1 cup Grana Padano cheese, grated
- 1 cup Colby cheese, shredded
- 2 tsp fresh chives, chopped
- 2 tbsp fresh parsley, chopped
- 1 garlic clove, minced

## Directions:

1. Using a bowl, combine the chicken with half of the marinara sauce, pepper, onion powder, Italian seasoning, salt, and 2 garlic cloves. In a separate bowl, combine the ricotta cheese with half of the Grana Padano cheese, chives, pepper, 1 garlic clove, half of the Colby cheese, salt, and 2 tablespoons parsley. Place half of the chicken mixture into a loaf pan, and spread evenly.
2. Place in cheese filling and spread evenly. Top with the rest of the meat mixture and spread again. Set the meatloaf in the oven at 380ºF and bake for 25 minutes. Remove meatloaf from oven, spread the rest of the marinara sauce, Grana Padano cheese and Colby cheese, and bake for 18 minutes. Allow meatloaf cooling and serve in slices sprinkled with 2 tbsp of chopped parsley.

## Nutrition Info:

- Info Per Servings 4g Carbs, 28g Protein, 14g Fat, 273 Calories

# Garlic & Ginger Chicken With Peanut Sauce

Servings: 6

Cooking Time: 1 Hour And 50 Minutes

## Ingredients:

- 1 tbsp wheat-free soy sauce
- 1 tbsp sugar-free fish sauce
- 1 tbsp lime juice
- 1 tsp cilantro
- 1 tsp minced garlic
- 1 tsp minced ginger
- 1 tbsp olive oil
- 1 tbsp rice wine vinegar
- 1 tsp cayenne pepper
- 1 tsp erythritol
- 6 chicken thighs
- Sauce:
- ½ cup peanut butter
- 1 tsp minced garlic
- 1 tbsp lime juice
- 2 tbsp water
- 1 tsp minced ginger
- 1 tbsp chopped jalapeño
- 2 tbsp rice wine vinegar
- 2 tbsp erythritol
- 1 tbsp fish sauce

## Directions:

1. Combine all chicken ingredients in a large Ziploc bag. Seal the bag and shake to combine. Refrigerate for 1 hour. Remove from fridge about 15 minutes before cooking.
2. Preheat the grill to medium and grill the chicken for 7 minutes per side. Whisk together all sauce ingredients in a mixing bowl. Serve the chicken drizzled with peanut sauce.

## Nutrition Info:

- Info Per Servings 3g Carbs, 35g Protein, 36g Fat, 492 Calories

# Greek Chicken With Capers

Servings: 4

Cooking Time: 30 Minutes

**Ingredients:**

- ¼ cup olive oil
- 1 onion, chopped
- 4 chicken breasts, skinless and boneless
- 4 garlic cloves, minced
- Salt and ground black pepper, to taste
- ½ cup kalamata olives, pitted and chopped
- 1 tbsp capers
- 1 pound tomatoes, chopped
- ½ tsp red chili flakes

**Directions:**

1. Sprinkle pepper and salt on the chicken, and rub with half of the oil. Add the chicken to a pan set over high heat, cook for 2 minutes, flip to the other side, and cook for 2 more minutes. Set the chicken breasts in the oven at 450ºF and bake for 8 minutes. Split the chicken into serving plates.
2. Set the same pan over medium heat and warm the remaining oil, place in the onion, olives, capers, garlic, and chili flakes, and cook for 1 minute. Stir in the tomatoes, pepper, and salt, and cook for 2 minutes. Sprinkle over the chicken breasts and enjoy.

**Nutrition Info:**

- Info Per Servings 2.2g Carbs, 25g Protein, 21g Fat, 387 Calories

# Eggplant & Tomato Braised Chicken Thighs

Servings: 4

Cooking Time: 45 Minutes

**Ingredients:**

- 2 tbsp ghee
- 1 lb chicken thighs
- Pink salt and black pepper to taste
- 2 cloves garlic, minced
- 1 can whole tomatoes
- 1 eggplant, diced
- 10 fresh basil leaves, chopped + extra to garnish

**Directions:**

1. Melt ghee in a saucepan over medium heat, season the chicken with salt and black pepper, and fry for 4 minutes on each side until golden brown. Remove chicken onto a plate.
2. Sauté the garlic in the ghee for 2 minutes, pour in the tomatoes, and cook covered for 8 minutes.
3. Add in the eggplant and basil. Cook for 4 minutes. Season the sauce with salt and black pepper, stir and add the chicken. Coat with sauce and simmer for 3 minutes.
4. Serve chicken with sauce on a bed of squash pasta. Garnish with extra basil.

**Nutrition Info:**

- Info Per Servings 2g Carbs, 26g Protein, 39.5g Fat, 468 Calories

# Lemon Chicken Bake

Servings: 6

Cooking Time: 55 Minutes

**Ingredients:**

- 6 skinless chicken breasts
- 1 parsnip, cut into wedges
- Salt and ground black pepper, to taste
- Juice from 2 lemons
- Zest from 2 lemons
- Lemon rinds from 2 lemons

**Directions:**

1. In a baking dish, add the chicken alongside pepper and salt. Sprinkle with lemon juice. Toss well to coat, place in parsnip, lemon rinds and lemon zest, set in an oven at 370ºF, and bake for 45 minutes.
2. Get rid of the lemon rinds, split the chicken onto plates, sprinkle sauce from the baking dish over.

**Nutrition Info:**

- Info Per Servings 4.5g Carbs, 25g Protein, 9g Fat, 274 Calories

# Easy Asian Chicken

Servings: 5

Cooking Time: 16 Minutes

**Ingredients:**

- 1 ½ lb. boneless chicken breasts, sliced into strips
- 1 tbsp ginger slices
- 3 tbsp coconut aminos
- ¼ cup organic chicken broth
- 3 cloves of garlic, minced
- 5 tablespoons sesame oil

**Directions:**

1. On high fire, heat a heavy-bottomed pot for 2 minutes. Add oil to a pan and swirl to coat bottom and sides. Heat oil for a minute.
2. Add garlic and ginger sauté for a minute.
3. Stir in chicken breast and sauté for 5 minutes. Season with coconut aminos and sauté for another 2 minutes.
4. Add remaining ingredients and bring to a boil.
5. Let it boil for 5 minutes.
6. Serve and enjoy.

**Nutrition Info:**

- Info Per Servings 1.2g Carbs, 30.9g Protein, 17.6g Fat, 299 Calories

# Chicken And Bacon Rolls

Servings: 4

Cooking Time: 45 Minutes

**Ingredients:**

- 1 tbsp fresh chives, chopped
- 8 ounces blue cheese
- 2 pounds chicken breasts, skinless, boneless, halved
- 12 bacon slices
- 2 tomatoes, chopped
- Salt and ground black pepper, to taste

**Directions:**

1. Set a pan over medium heat, place in the bacon, cook until halfway done, remove to paper towels, and drain the grease. Using a bowl, stir together the blue cheese, chives, tomatoes, pepper, and salt.
2. Use a meat tenderizer to flatten the chicken breasts well, season and lay the cream cheese mixture on top. Roll them up, and wrap each in a bacon slice. Place the wrapped chicken breasts in a greased baking dish, and roast in the oven at 370ºF for 30 minutes. Serve on top of wilted kale.

**Nutrition Info:**

- Info Per Servings 5g Carbs, 38g Protein, 48g Fat, 623 Calories

# Turkey & Cheese Stuffed Mushrooms

Servings: 5

Cooking Time: 20 Minutes

**Ingredients:**

- 12 ounces button mushroom caps
- 3 ounces cream cheese
- ¼ cup carrot, chopped
- 1 tsp ranch seasoning mix
- 4 tbsp hot sauce
- ¾ cup blue cheese, crumbled
- ¼ cup onion, chopped
- ½ cup turkey breasts, cooked, chopped
- Salt and black pepper, to taste
- Cooking spray

**Directions:**

1. Using a bowl, combine the cream cheese with the blue cheese, ranch seasoning, turkey, onion, carrot, salt, hot sauce, and pepper. Stuff each mushroom cap with this mixture, set on a lined baking sheet, spray with cooking spray, place in the oven at 425ºF, and bake for 10 minutes.

**Nutrition Info:**

- Info Per Servings 8.6g Carbs, 51g Protein, 17g Fat, 486 Calories

# Chicken With Monterey Jack Cheese

Servings: 3

Cooking Time: 30 Minutes

**Ingredients:**

- 2 tbsp butter
- 1 tsp garlic, minced
- 1 pound chicken breasts
- 1 tsp creole seasoning
- ¼ cup scallions, chopped
- ½ cup tomatoes, chopped
- ½ cup chicken stock
- ¼ cup whipping cream
- ½ cup Monterey Jack cheese, grated
- ¼ cup fresh cilantro, chopped
- Salt and black pepper, to taste
- 4 ounces cream cheese
- 8 eggs
- A pinch of garlic powder

**Directions:**

1. Set a pan over medium heat and warm 1 tbsp butter. Add chicken, season with creole seasoning and cook each side for 2 minutes; remove to a plate. Melt the rest of the butter and stir in garlic and tomatoes; cook for 4 minutes. Return the chicken to the pan and pour in stock; cook for 15 minutes. Place in whipping cream, scallions, salt, Monterey Jack cheese, and pepper; cook for 2 minutes.
2. In a blender, combine the cream cheese with garlic powder, salt, eggs, and pepper, and pulse well. Place the mixture into a lined baking sheet, and then bake for 10 minutes in the oven at 325°F. Allow the cheese sheet to cool down, place on a cutting board, roll, and slice into medium slices. Split the slices among bowls and top with chicken mixture. Sprinkle with chopped cilantro to serve.

**Nutrition Info:**

- Info Per Servings 4g Carbs, 39g Protein, 34g Fat, 445 Calories

# Homemade Chicken Pizza Calzone

Servings: 4

Cooking Time: 60 Minutes

**Ingredients:**

- 2 eggs
- 1 low carb pizza crust
- ½ cup Pecorino cheese, grated
- 1 lb chicken breasts, skinless, boneless, halved
- ½ cup sugar-free marinara sauce
- 1 tsp Italian seasoning
- 1 tsp onion powder
- 1 tsp garlic powder
- Salt and black pepper, to taste
- ¼ cup flax seed, ground
- 6 ounces provolone cheese

**Directions:**

1. Using a bowl, combine the Italian seasoning with onion powder, salt, Pecorino cheese, pepper, garlic powder, and flax seed. In a separate bowl, combine the eggs with pepper and salt.
2. Dip the chicken pieces in eggs, and then in seasoning mixture, lay all parts on a lined baking sheet, and bake for 25 minutes in the oven at 390° F.
3. Place the pizza crust dough on a lined baking sheet and spread half of the provolone cheese on half. Remove chicken from oven, chop it, and scatter it over the provolone cheese. Spread over the marinara sauce and top with the remaining cheese.
4. Cover with the other half of the dough and shape the pizza in a calzone. Seal the edges, set in the oven and bake for 20 minutes. Allow the calzone to cool down before slicing and enjoy.

**Nutrition Info:**

- Info Per Servings 4.6g Carbs, 28g Protein, 15g Fat, 425 Calories

# Yummy Chicken Nuggets

Servings: 2

Cooking Time: 25 Minutes

**Ingredients:**

- ½ cup almond flour
- 1 egg
- 2 tbsp garlic powder
- 2 chicken breasts, cubed
- Salt and black pepper, to taste
- ½ cup butter

**Directions:**

1. Using a bowl, combine salt, garlic powder, flour, and pepper, and stir. In a separate bowl, beat the egg. Add the chicken breast cubes in egg mixture, then in the flour mixture. Set a pan over medium-high heat and warm butter, add in the chicken nuggets, and cook for 6 minutes on each side. Remove to paper towels, drain the excess grease and serve.

**Nutrition Info:**

- Info Per Servings 4.3g Carbs, 35g Protein, 37g Fat, 417 Calories

# Chicken And Spinach Stir Fry

Servings: 4

Cooking Time: 10 Minutes

**Ingredients:**

- 2 cloves of garlic, minced
- 1 tablespoon fresh ginger, grated
- 1 ¼ pounds boneless chicken breasts, cut into strips
- 2 tablespoons yellow miso, diluted in water
- 2 cups baby spinach
- 2 tablespoons olive oil
- Pepper and salt to taste

**Directions:**

1. Heat oil in a skillet over medium-high heat and sauté the garlic for 30 seconds until fragrant.

2. Stir in the ginger and chicken breasts. Season lightly with pepper and salt.
3. Cook for 5 minutes while stirring constantly.
4. Stir in the diluted miso paste.
5. Continue cooking for 3 more minutes before adding spinach.
6. Cook for another minute or until the spinach leaves have wilted.

**Nutrition Info:**

- Info Per Servings 1.3g Carbs, 32.5g Protein, 10.5g Fat, 237 Calories

# Red Wine Chicken

Servings: 4

Cooking Time: 30 Minutes

**Ingredients:**

- 3 tbsp coconut oil
- 2 lb chicken breast halves, skinless and boneless
- 3 garlic cloves, minced
- Salt and black pepper, to taste
- 1 cup chicken stock
- 3 tbsp stevia
- ½ cup red wine
- 2 tomatoes, sliced
- 6 mozzarella slices
- Fresh basil, chopped, for serving

**Directions:**

1. Set a pan over medium-high heat and warm oil, add the chicken, season with pepper and salt, cook until brown. Stir in the stevia, garlic, stock, and red wine, and cook for 10 minutes.
2. Remove to a lined baking sheet and arrange mozzarella cheese slices on top. Broil in the oven over medium heat until cheese melts and lay tomato slices over chicken pieces.
3. Sprinkle with chopped basil to serve.

**Nutrition Info:**

- Info Per Servings 4g Carbs, 27g Protein, 12g Fat, 314 Calories

# Cheddar Chicken Tenders

Servings: 4

Cooking Time: 40 Minutes

**Ingredients:**

- 2 eggs
- 3 tbsp butter, melted
- 3 cups coarsely crushed cheddar cheese
- ½ cup pork rinds, crushed
- 1 lb chicken tenders
- Pink salt to taste

**Directions:**

1. Preheat oven to 350ºF and line a baking sheet with parchment paper. Whisk the eggs with the butter in one bowl and mix the cheese and pork rinds in another bowl.
2. Season chicken with salt, dip in egg mixture, and coat generously in cheddar mixture. Place on baking sheet, cover with aluminium foil and bake for 25 minutes. Remove foil and bake further for 12 minutes to golden brown. Serve chicken with mustard dip.

**Nutrition Info:**

- Info Per Servings 1.3g Carbs, 42g Protein, 54g Fat, 507 Calories

# Turkey & Leek Soup

Servings: 4

Cooking Time: 45 Minutes

**Ingredients:**

- 3 celery stalks, chopped
- 2 leeks, chopped
- 1 tbsp butter
- 6 cups chicken stock
- Salt and ground black pepper, to taste
- ¼ cup fresh parsley, chopped
- 3 cups zoodles
- 3 cups turkey meat, cooked and chopped

**Directions:**

1. Set a pot over medium-high heat, stir in leeks and celery and cook for 5 minutes. Place in the parsley, turkey meat, pepper, salt, and stock, and cook for 20 minutes. Stir in the zoodles, and cook turkey soup for 5 minutes. Serve in bowls and enjoy.

**Nutrition Info:**

- Info Per Servings 3g Carbs, 15g Protein, 11g Fat, 305 Calories

# Chicken Breasts With Cheddar & Pepperoni

Servings: 4

Cooking Time: 40 Minutes

**Ingredients:**

- 12 oz canned tomato sauce
- 1 tbsp olive oil
- 4 chicken breast halves, skinless and boneless
- Salt and ground black pepper, to taste
- 1 tsp dried oregano
- 4 oz cheddar cheese, sliced
- 1 tsp garlic powder
- 2 oz pepperoni, sliced

**Directions:**

1. Preheat your oven to 390ºF. Using a bowl, combine chicken with oregano, salt, garlic, and pepper.
2. Heat a pan with the olive oil over medium-high heat, add in the chicken, cook each side for 2 minutes, and remove to a baking dish. Top with the cheddar cheese slices spread the sauce, then cover with pepperoni slices. Bake for 30 minutes. Serve warm garnished with fresh oregano if desired

**Nutrition Info:**

- Info Per Servings 4.5g Carbs, 32g Protein, 21g Fat, 387 Calories

## Basil Turkey Meatballs

Servings: 4

Cooking Time: 15 Minutes

**Ingredients:**

- 1 pound ground turkey
- 2 tbsp chopped sun-dried tomatoes
- 2 tbsp chopped basil
- ½ tsp garlic powder
- 1 egg
- ½ tsp salt
- ¼ cup almond flour
- 2 tbsp olive oil
- ½ cup shredded mozzarella
- ¼ tsp pepper

**Directions:**

1. Place everything except the oil in a bowl. Mix with your hands until combined. Form 16 meatballs out of the mixture. Heat the olive oil in a skillet over medium heat. Cook the meatballs for 3 minutes per each side.

**Nutrition Info:**

- Info Per Servings 2g Carbs, 22g Protein, 26g Fat, 310 Calories

## Almond-crusted Chicken Breasts

Servings: 4

Cooking Time: 60 Minutes

**Ingredients:**

- 4 bacon slices, cooked and crumbled
- 4 chicken breasts
- 1 tbsp water
- ½ cup olive oil
- 1 egg, whisked
- Salt and black pepper, to taste
- 1 cup asiago cheese, shredded
- ¼ tsp garlic powder
- 1 cup ground almonds

**Directions:**

1. Using a bowl, combine the ground almonds with pepper, salt, and garlic. Place the whisked egg in a separate bowl and combine with water. Apply a seasoning of pepper and salt to the chicken, and dip each piece into the egg, and then into almond mixture.
2. Set a pan over medium-high heat and warm oil, add in the chicken breasts, cook until are golden-brown, and remove to a baking pan. Bake in the oven at 360ºF for 20 minutes. Scatter with Asiago cheese and bacon and return to the oven. Roast for a few minutes until the cheese melts.

**Nutrition Info:**

- Info Per Servings 1g Carbs, 41g Protein, 32g Fat, 485 Calories

## Heart Healthy Chicken Salad

Servings: 4

Cooking Time: 45 Minutes

**Ingredients:**

- 3 tbsp mayonnaise, low-fat
- ½ tsp onion powder
- 1 tbsp lemon juice
- ¼ cup celery (chopped)
- 3 ¼ cups chicken breast (cooked, cubed, and skinless)
- Salt and pepper to taste

**Directions:**

1. Bake chicken breasts for 45 minutes at 350oF. Let it cool and cut them into cubes and place them in the refrigerator.
2. Combine all other ingredients in a large bowl then add the chilled chicken.
3. Mix well and ready to serve.
4. Enjoy!

**Nutrition Info:**

- Info Per Servings 1.0g Carbs, 50.0g Protein, 22.0g Fat, 408 Calories

# Chicken, Broccoli & Cashew Stir-fry

Servings: 4

Cooking Time: 30 Minutes

**Ingredients:**

- 2 chicken breasts, cut into strips
- 3 tbsp olive oil
- 2 tbsp soy sauce
- 2 tsp white wine vinegar
- 1 tsp erythritol
- 2 tsp xanthan gum
- 1 lemon, juiced
- 1 cup unsalted cashew nuts
- 2 cups broccoli florets
- 1 white onion, thinly sliced
- Pepper to taste

**Directions:**

1. In a bowl, mix the soy sauce, vinegar, lemon juice, erythritol, and xanthan gum. Set aside.
2. Heat the oil in a wok and fry the cashew for 4 minutes until golden-brown. Remove the cashews into a paper towel lined plate and set aside. Sauté the onion in the same oil for 4 minutes until soft and browned; add to the cashew nuts.
3. Add the chicken to the wok and cook for 4 minutes; include the broccoli and pepper. Stir-fry and pour the soy sauce mixture in. Stir and cook the sauce for 4 minutes and pour in the cashews and onion. Stir once more, cook for 1 minute, and turn the heat off.
4. Serve the chicken stir-fry with some steamed cauli rice.

**Nutrition Info:**

- Info Per Servings 3.4g Carbs, 17.3g Protein, 10.1g Fat, 286 Calories

# Chicken With Parmesan Topping

Servings: 4

Cooking Time: 45 Minutes

**Ingredients:**

- 4 chicken breast halves, skinless and boneless
- Salt and black pepper, to taste
- ¼ cup green chilies, chopped
- 5 bacon slices, chopped
- 8 ounces cream cheese
- ¼ cup onion, peeled and chopped
- ½ cup mayonnaise
- ½ cup Grana Padano cheese, grated
- 1 cup cheddar cheese, grated
- 2 ounces pork skins, crushed
- 4 tbsp melted butter
- ½ cup Parmesan cheese

**Directions:**

1. Lay the chicken breasts in a baking dish, season with pepper, and salt, place in the oven at 420ºF and bake for 30 minutes. Set a pan over medium heat, add in the bacon, cook until crispy and remove to a plate. Stir in the onion, and cook for 3 minutes.
2. Remove from heat, add in bacon, cream cheese, ½ cup Grana Padano, mayonnaise, chilies, and cheddar cheese, and spread over the chicken. In a bowl, combine the pork skin with ½ cup Parmesan cheese, and butter. Spread over the chicken as well, place in an oven, and bake for 10 minutes.

**Nutrition Info:**

- Info Per Servings 5g Carbs, 25g Protein, 15g Fat, 361 Calories

# Vegan, Vegetable & Meatless Recipes

# Vegan, Vegetable & Meatless Recipes

## Greek Styled Veggie-rice

Servings: 3

Cooking Time: 20 Minutes

**Ingredients:**

- 3 tbsp chopped fresh mint
- 1 small tomato, chopped
- 1 head cauliflower, cut into large florets
- ¼ cup fresh lemon juice
- ½ yellow onion, minced
- pepper and salt to taste
- ¼ cup extra virgin olive oil

**Directions:**

1. In a bowl, mix lemon juice and onion and leave for 30 minutes. Then drain onion and reserve the juice and onion bits.
2. In a blender, shred cauliflower until the size of a grain of rice.
3. On medium fire, place a medium nonstick skillet and for 8-10 minutes cook cauliflower while covered.
4. Add grape tomatoes and cook for 3 minutes while stirring occasionally.
5. Add mint and onion bits. Cook for another three minutes.
6. Meanwhile, in a small bowl whisk pepper, salt, 3 tbsp reserved lemon juice, and olive oil until well blended.
7. Remove cooked cauliflower, transfer to a serving bowl, pour lemon juice mixture, and toss to mix.
8. Before serving, if needed season with pepper and salt to taste.

**Nutrition Info:**

- Info Per Servings 4.0g Carbs, 2.3g Protein, 9.5g Fat, 120 Calories

## Smoked Tofu With Rosemary Sauce

Servings: 4

Cooking Time: 20 Minutes

**Ingredients:**

- 10 ounces smoked tofu, pressed and drained
- 2 tbsp sesame oil
- 1 onion, chopped
- 1 tsp garlic, minced
- ½ cup vegetable broth
- ½ tsp turmeric powder
- Sea salt and black pepper, to taste
- For the Sauce
- ½ tbsp olive oil
- 1 cup tomato sauce
- 2 tbsp white wine
- 1 tsp fresh rosemary, chopped
- 1 tsp chili garlic sauce

**Directions:**

1. Pat dry the tofu using a paper towel and chop into 1-inch cubes. Set a frying pan over medium-high heat and warm sesame oil. Add in the tofu cubes and fry until browned. Stir in salt, broth, pepper, garlic, turmeric powder, and onions. Cook until all liquid evaporates.
2. As the process goes on, you can prepare the sauce. Set a pan over medium-high heat and warm olive oil. Place in tomato sauce and heat until cooked through.
3. Place in the rest of the ingredients and simmer for 10 minutes over medium heat approximately 10 minutes. Divide in serving bowls and serve alongside prepared tofu cubes!

**Nutrition Info:**

- Info Per Servings 9.3g Carbs, 27.6g Protein, 22.2g Fat, 336 Calories

## Herb Butter With Parsley

Servings: 1

Cooking Time: 0 Minutes

**Ingredients:**

- 5 oz. butter, at room temperature
- 1 garlic clove, pressed
- ½ tbsp garlic powder
- 4 tbsp fresh parsley, finely chopped
- 1 tsp lemon juice
- ½ tsp salt

**Directions:**

1. In a bowl, stir all ingredients until completely combined. Set aside for 15 minutes or refrigerate it before serving.

**Nutrition Info:**

- Info Per Servings 1g Carbs, 1g Protein, 28g Fat, 258 Calories

## Grilled Parmesan Eggplant

Servings: 4

Cooking Time: 15 Minutes

**Ingredients:**

- 1 medium-sized eggplant
- 1 log fresh mozzarella cheese, cut into sixteen slices
- 1 small tomato, cut into eight slices
- 1/2 cup shredded Parmesan cheese
- Chopped fresh basil or parsley
- 1/2 teaspoon salt
- 1 tablespoon olive oil
- 1/2 teaspoon pepper

**Directions:**

1. Trim ends of the eggplant; cut eggplant crosswise into eight slices. Sprinkle with salt; let stand 5 minutes.
2. Blot eggplant dry with paper towels; brush both sides with oil and sprinkle with pepper. Grill, covered, over medium heat 4-6 minutes on each side

or until tender. Remove from grill.

3. Top eggplant with mozzarella cheese, tomato, and Parmesan cheese. Grill, covered, 1-2 minutes longer or until cheese begins to melt. Top with basil.

**Nutrition Info:**

- Info Per Servings 10g Carbs, 26g Protein, 31g Fat, 449 Calories

## Sriracha Tofu With Yogurt Sauce

Servings: 4

Cooking Time: 40 Minutes

**Ingredients:**

- 12 ounces tofu, pressed and sliced
- 1 cup green onions, chopped
- 1 garlic clove, minced
- 2 tbsp vinegar
- 1 tbsp sriracha sauce
- 2 tbsp olive oil
- For Yogurt Sauce
- 2 cloves garlic, pressed
- 2 tbsp fresh lemon juice
- Sea salt and black pepper, to taste
- 1 tsp fresh dill weed
- 1 cup Greek yogurt
- 1 cucumber, shredded

**Directions:**

1. Put tofu slices, garlic, Sriracha sauce, vinegar, and scallions in a bowl; allow to settle for approximately 30 minutes. Set oven to medium-high heat and add oil in a nonstick skillet to warm. Cook tofu for 5 minutes until golden brown.
2. For the preparation of sauce, use a bowl to mix garlic, salt, yogurt, black pepper, lemon juice, and dill. Add in shredded cucumber as you stir to combine well. Put the yogurt sauce in your fridge until ready to serve. Serve the tofu in serving plates with a dollop of yogurt sauce.

**Nutrition Info:**

- Info Per Servings 8.1g Carbs, 17.5g Protein, 25.9g Fat, 351 Calories

# Grated Cauliflower With Seasoned Mayo

Servings: 2

Cooking Time: 15 Mins

**Ingredients:**

- 1 lb grated cauliflower
- 3 oz. butter
- 4 eggs
- 3 oz. pimientos de padron or poblano peppers
- ½ cup mayonnaise
- 1 tsp olive oil
- Salt and pepper
- 1 tsp garlic powder (optional)

**Directions:**

1. In a bowl, whisk together the mayonnaise and garlic and set aside.
2. Rinse, trim and grate the cauliflower using a food processor or grater.
3. Melt a generous amount of butter and fry grated cauliflower for about 5 minutes. Season salt and pepper to taste.
4. Fry poblanos with oil until lightly crispy. Then fry eggs as you want and sprinkle salt and pepper over them.
5. Serve with poblanos and cauliflower. Drizzle some mayo mixture on top.

**Nutrition Info:**

- Info Per Servings 9g Carbs, 17g Protein, 87g Fat, 898 Calories

# Roasted Brussels Sprouts With Sunflower Seeds

Servings: 6

Cooking Time: 45 Minutes

**Ingredients:**

- Nonstick cooking spray
- 3 pounds brussels sprouts, halved
- ¼ cup olive oil
- Salt and ground black pepper, to taste
- 1 tsp sunflower seeds
- 2 tbsp fresh chives, chopped

**Directions:**

1. Set oven to 390ºF. Apply a nonstick cooking spray to a rimmed baking sheet. Arrange sprout halves on the baking sheet. Shake in black pepper, salt, sunflower seeds, and olive oil.
2. Roast for 40 minutes, until the cabbage becomes soft. Apply a garnish of fresh chopped chives.

**Nutrition Info:**

- Info Per Servings 8g Carbs, 2.1g Protein, 17g Fat, 186 Calories

# Keto Enchilada Bake

Servings: 6

Cooking Time: 20 Minutes

**Ingredients:**

- 1 package House Foods Organic Extra Firm Tofu
- 1 cup roma tomatoes, chopped
- 1 cup shredded cheddar cheese
- 1 small avocado, pitted and sliced
- ½ cup sour cream
- 5 tablespoons olive oil
- Salt and pepper to taste

**Directions:**

1. Preheat oven to 350F.
2. Cut tofu into small cubes and sauté with oil and seasoning. Set aside and reserve the oil.
3. Place the tofu in the bottom of a casserole dish.
4. Mix the reserved oil and tomatoes and pour over the tofu.
5. Sprinkle with cheese on top.
6. Bake for 20 minutes.
7. Top with avocado and sour cream toppings.
8. Serve and enjoy.

**Nutrition Info:**

- Info Per Servings 6g Carbs, 38g Protein, 40g Fat, 568 Calories

# Vegan Cheesy Chips With Tomatoes

Servings: 6

Cooking Time: 15 Minutes

**Ingredients:**

- 5 tomatoes, sliced
- ¼ cup olive oil
- 1 tbsp seasoning mix
- For Vegan cheese
- ½ cup pepitas seeds
- 1 tbsp nutritional yeast
- Salt and black pepper, to taste
- 1 tsp garlic puree

**Directions:**

1. Over the sliced tomatoes, drizzle olive oil. Set oven to 200ºF.
2. In a food processor, add all vegan cheese ingredients and pulse until the desired consistency is attained. Combine vegan cheese and seasoning mixture. Toss in seasoned tomato slices to coat.
3. Set the tomato slices on the prepared baking pan and bake for 10 minutes.

**Nutrition Info:**

- Info Per Servings 7.2g Carbs, 4.6g Protein, 14g Fat, 161 Calories

## Easy Vanilla Granola

Servings: 6

Cooking Time: 1 Hour

**Ingredients:**

- ½ cup hazelnuts, chopped
- 1 cup walnuts, chopped
- ⅓ cup flax meal
- ⅓ cup coconut milk
- ⅓ cup poppy seeds
- ⅓ cup pumpkin seeds
- 8 drops stevia
- ⅓ cup coconut oil, melted
- 1 ½ tsp vanilla paste

- 1 tsp ground cloves
- 1 tsp grated nutmeg
- 1 tsp lemon zest
- ⅓ cup water

**Directions:**

1. Set oven to 300ºF. Line a parchment paper to a baking sheet. Combine all ingredients. Spread the mixture onto the baking sheet in an even layer. Bake for 55 minutes, as you stir at intervals of 15 minutes. Let cool at room temperature.

**Nutrition Info:**

- Info Per Servings 5.1g Carbs, 9.3g Protein, 44.9g Fat, 449 Calories

## Garlic And Greens

Servings: 4

Cooking Time: 20 Minutes

**Ingredients:**

- 1-pound kale, trimmed and torn
- 1/4 cup chopped oil-packed sun-dried tomatoes
- 5 garlic cloves, minced
- 2 tablespoons minced fresh parsley
- 1/4 teaspoon salt
- 3 tablespoons olive oil

**Directions:**

1. In a 6-qt. stockpot, bring 1 inch. of water to a boil. Add kale; cook, covered, 10-15 minutes or until tender. Remove with a slotted spoon; discard cooking liquid.
2. In the same pot, heat oil over medium heat. Add tomatoes and garlic; cook and stir 1 minute. Add kale, parsley and salt; heat through, stirring occasionally.

**Nutrition Info:**

- Info Per Servings 9g Carbs, 6g Protein, 13g Fat, 160 Calories

# Cauliflower & Mushrooms Stuffed Peppers

Servings: 4

Cooking Time: 40 Minutes

**Ingredients:**

- 1 head cauliflower
- 4 bell peppers
- 1 cup mushrooms, sliced
- 1 ½ tbsp oil
- 1 onion, chopped
- 1 cup celery, chopped
- 1 garlic cloves, minced
- 1 tsp chili powder
- 2 tomatoes, pureed
- Sea salt and pepper, to taste

**Directions:**

1. To prepare cauliflower rice, grate the cauliflower into rice-size. Set in a kitchen towel to attract and remove any excess moisture. Set oven to 360ºF.
2. Lightly oil a casserole dish. Chop off bell pepper tops, do away with the seeds and core. Line a baking pan with a parchment paper and roast the peppers for 18 minutes until the skin starts to brown.
3. Warm the oil over medium heat. Add in garlic, celery, and onion and sauté until soft and translucent.Stir in chili powder, mushrooms, and cauliflower rice. Cook for 6 minutes until the cauliflower rice becomes tender. Split the cauliflower mixture among the bell peppers. Set in the casserole dish.Combine pepper, salt, and tomatoes. Top the peppers with the tomato mixture. Bake for 10 minutes.

**Nutrition Info:**

- Info Per Servings 8.4g Carbs, 1.6g Protein, 4.8g Fat, 77 Calories

# Mushroom & Jalapeño Stew

Servings: 4

Cooking Time: 50 Minutes

**Ingredients:**

- 2 tsp olive oil
- 1 cup leeks, chopped
- 1 garlic clove, minced
- ½ cup celery, chopped
- ½ cup carrot, chopped
- 1 green bell pepper, chopped
- 1 jalapeño pepper, chopped
- 2 ½ cups mushrooms, sliced
- 1 ½ cups vegetable stock
- 2 tomatoes, chopped
- 2 thyme sprigs, chopped
- 1 rosemary sprig, chopped
- 2 bay leaves
- ½ tsp salt
- ¼ tsp ground black pepper
- 2 tbsp vinegar

**Directions:**

1. Set a pot over medium-high heat and warm oil. Add in garlic and leeks and sauté until soft and translucent. Add in the pepper, celery, mushrooms, and carrots.
2. Cook as you stir for 12 minutes; stir in a splash of vegetable stock to ensure there is no sticking. Stir in the rest of the ingredients. Set heat to medium; allow to simmer for 25 to 35 minutes or until cooked through. Divide into individual bowls and serve while warm.

**Nutrition Info:**

- Info Per Servings 9g Carbs, 2.7g Protein, 2.7g Fat, 65 Calories

# Brussels Sprouts With Tofu

Servings: 4

Cooking Time: 20 Minutes

**Ingredients:**

- 2 tbsp olive oil
- 2 garlic cloves, minced
- ½ cup onion, chopped
- 10 ounces tofu, crumbled
- 2 tbsp water
- 2 tbsp soy sauce
- 1 tbsp tomato puree
- ½ pound Brussels sprouts, quartered
- Sea salt and black pepper, to taste

**Directions:**

1. Set a saucepan over medium-high heat and warm the oil. Add onion and garlic and cook until tender. Place in the soy sauce, water, and tofu. Cook for 5 minutes until the tofu starts to brown.
2. Add in brussels sprouts; apply pepper and salt for seasoning; reduce heat to low and cook for 13 minutes while stirring frequently. Serve while warm.

**Nutrition Info:**

- Info Per Servings 12.1g Carbs, 10.5g Protein, 11.7g Fat, 179 Calories

# Vegan Mushroom Pizza

Servings: 4

Cooking Time: 35 Minutes

**Ingredients:**

- 2 tsp ghee
- 1 cup chopped button mushrooms
- ½ cup sliced mixed colored bell peppers
- Pink salt and black pepper to taste
- 1 almond flour pizza bread
- 1 cup tomato sauce
- 1 tsp vegan Parmesan cheese
- Vegan Parmesan cheese for garnish

**Directions:**

1. Melt ghee in a skillet over medium heat, sauté the mushrooms and bell peppers for 10 minutes to soften. Season with salt and black pepper. Turn the heat off.
2. Put the pizza bread on a pizza pan, spread the tomato sauce all over the top and scatter vegetables evenly on top. Season with a little more salt and sprinkle with parmesan cheese.
3. Bake for 20 minutes until the vegetables are soft and the cheese has melted and is bubbly. Garnish with extra parmesan cheese. Slice pizza and serve with chilled berry juice.

**Nutrition Info:**

- Info Per Servings 8g Carbs, 15g Protein, 20g Fat, 295 Calories

# Cilantro-lime Guacamole

Servings: 4

Cooking Time: 10 Minutes

**Ingredients:**

- 3 avocados, peeled, pitted, and mashed
- 1 lime, juiced
- 1/2 cup diced onion
- 3 tablespoons chopped fresh cilantro
- 2 Roma (plum) tomatoes, diced
- 1 teaspoon salt
- 1 teaspoon minced garlic
- 1 pinch ground cayenne pepper (optional)
- 1 teaspoon minced garlic

**Directions:**

1. In a mixing bowl, mash the avocados with a fork. Sprinkle with salt and lime juice.
2. Stir together diced onion, tomatoes, cilantro, pepper and garlic.
3. Serve immediately, or refrigerate until ready to serve.

**Nutrition Info:**

- Info Per Servings 8g Carbs, 19g Protein, 22.2g Fat, 362 Calories

# Tofu Sandwich With Cabbage Slaw

Servings: 4

Cooking Time: 4 Hours 10 Minutes

**Ingredients:**

- ½ lb Firm tofu, sliced
- 4 low carb buns
- 1 tbsp olive oil
- Marinade
- Salt and black pepper to taste
- 2 tsp allspice
- 1 tbsp erythritol
- 2 tsp chopped thyme
- 1 Habanero, seeded and minced
- 3 green onions, thinly sliced
- 2 cloves garlic
- ¼ cup olive oil
- Slaw
- ½ small cabbage, shredded
- 1 carrot, grated
- ½ red onion, grated
- 2 tsp swerve
- 2 tbsp white vinegar
- 1 pinch Italian seasoning
- ¼ cup olive oil
- 1 tsp Dijon mustard
- Salt and black pepper to taste

**Directions:**

1. In a food processor, make the marinade by blending the allspice, salt, black pepper, erythritol, thyme, habanero, green onions, garlic, and olive oil, for a minute. Pour the mixture in a bowl and put the tofu in it, coating it to be covered with marinade. Place in the fridge to marinate for 4 hours.
2. Make the slaw next: In a large bowl, evenly combine the white vinegar, swerve, olive oil, Dijon mustard, Italian seasoning, salt, and pepper. Stir in the cabbage, carrot, and onion, and place it in the refrigerator to chill while the tofu marinates.
3. Frying the tofu: heat 1 teaspoon of oil in a skillet over medium heat, remove the tofu from the marinade, and cook it in the oil to brown on both sides for 6 minutes in total. Remove onto a plate after

and toast the buns in the skillet. In the buns, add the tofu and top with the slaw. Close the bread and serve with a sweet chili sauce.

**Nutrition Info:**

- Info Per Servings 7.8g Carbs, 14g Protein, 33g Fat, 386 Calories

# Briam With Tomato Sauce

Servings: 4

Cooking Time: 70 Minutes

**Ingredients:**

- 3 tbsp olive oil
- 1 large eggplant, halved and sliced
- 1 large onion, thinly sliced
- 3 cloves garlic, sliced
- 5 tomatoes, diced
- 3 rutabagas, peeled and diced
- 1 cup sugar-free tomato sauce
- 4 zucchinis, sliced
- ¼ cup water
- Salt and black pepper to taste
- 1 tbsp dried oregano
- 2 tbsp chopped parsley

**Directions:**

1. Preheat the oven to 400ºF. Heat the olive oil in a skillet over medium heat and cook the eggplants in it for 6 minutes to brown on the edges. After, remove to a medium bowl.
2. Sauté the onion and garlic in the oil for 3 minutes and add them to the eggplants. Turn the heat off.
3. In the eggplants bowl, mix in the tomatoes, rutabagas, tomato sauce, and zucchinis. Add the water and stir in the salt, pepper, oregano, and parsley. Pour the mixture in the casserole dish. Place the dish in the oven and bake for 45 to 60 minutes. Serve the briam warm on a bed of cauli rice.

**Nutrition Info:**

- Info Per Servings 12.5g Carbs, 11.3g Protein, 12g Fat, 365 Calories

# Garlic 'n Sour Cream Zucchini Bake

Servings: 3

Cooking Time: 35 Minutes

**Ingredients:**

- 1 ½ cups zucchini slices
- 5 tablespoons olive oil
- 1 tablespoon minced garlic
- 1/4 cup grated Parmesan cheese
- 1 package cream cheese, softened
- Salt and pepper to taste

**Directions:**

1. Lightly grease a baking sheet with cooking spray.
2. Place zucchini in a bowl and put in olive oil and garlic.
3. Place zucchini slices in a single layer in dish.
4. Bake for 35 minutes at 390oF until crispy.
5. In a bowl, whisk well, remaining ingredients.
6. Serve with zucchini

**Nutrition Info:**

- Info Per Servings 9.5g Carbs, 11.9g Protein, 32.4g Fat, 385 Calories

# Cheesy Cauliflower Falafel

Servings: 4

Cooking Time: 15 Minutes

**Ingredients:**

- 1 head cauliflower, cut into florets
- ⅓ cup silvered ground almonds
- ½ tsp mixed spice
- Salt and chili pepper to taste
- 3 tbsp coconut flour
- 3 fresh eggs
- 4 tbsp ghee

**Directions:**

1. Blend the cauli florets in a food processor until a grain meal consistency is formed. Pour the puree in a bowl, add the ground almonds, mixed spice, salt, chili pepper, and coconut flour, and mix until evenly combined.
2. Beat the eggs in a bowl until creamy in color and mix with the cauli mixture. Shape ¼ cup each into patties and set aside.
3. Melt ghee in a frying pan over medium heat and fry the patties for 5 minutes on each side to be firm and browned. Remove onto a wire rack to cool, share into serving plates, and top with tahini sauce.

**Nutrition Info:**

- Info Per Servings 2g Carbs, 8g Protein, 26g Fat, 315 Calories

# Cauliflower Risotto With Mushrooms

Servings: 4

Cooking Time: 15 Minutes

**Ingredients:**

- 2 shallots, diced
- 3 tbsp olive oil
- ¼ cup veggie broth
- ⅓ cup Parmesan cheese
- 4 tbsp butter
- 3 tbsp chopped chives
- 2 pounds mushrooms, sliced
- 4 ½ cups riced cauliflower

**Directions:**

1. Heat 2 tbsp. oil in a saucepan. Add the mushrooms and cook over medium heat for about 3 minutes. Remove from the pan and set aside.
2. Heat the remaining oil and cook the shallots for 2 minutes. Stir in the cauliflower and broth, and cook until the liquid is absorbed. Stir in the rest of the ingredients.

**Nutrition Info:**

- Info Per Servings 8.4g Carbs, 11g Protein, 18g Fat, 264 Calories

# Colorful Vegan Soup

Servings: 6

Cooking Time: 25 Minutes

**Ingredients:**

- 2 tsp olive oil
- 1 red onion, chopped
- 2 cloves garlic, minced
- 1 celery stalk, chopped
- 1 head broccoli, chopped
- 1 carrot, sliced
- 1 cup spinach, torn into pieces
- 1 cup collard greens, chopped
- Sea salt and black pepper, to taste
- 2 thyme sprigs, chopped
- 1 rosemary sprig, chopped
- 2 bay leaves
- 6 cups vegetable stock
- 2 tomatoes, chopped
- 1 cup almond milk
- 1 tbsp white miso paste
- ½ cup arugula

**Directions:**

1. Place a large pot over medium-high heat and warm oil. Add in carrots, celery, onion, broccoli, garlic, and sauté until soft.
2. Place in spinach, salt, rosemary, tomatoes, bay leaves, ground black pepper, collard greens, thyme, and vegetable stock. On low heat, simmer the mixture for 15 minutes while the lid is slightly open.
3. Stir in white miso paste, watercress, and almond milk and cook for 5 more minutes.

**Nutrition Info:**

- Info Per Servings 9g Carbs, 2.9g Protein, 11.4g Fat, 142 Calories

# Zucchini Lasagna With Ricotta And Spinach

Servings: 4

Cooking Time: 50 Minutes

**Ingredients:**

- Cooking spray
- 2 zucchinis, sliced
- Salt and black pepper to taste
- 2 cups ricotta cheese
- 2 cups shredded mozzarella cheese
- 3 cups tomato sauce
- 1 cup packed baby spinach

**Directions:**

1. Preheat oven to 370°F and grease a baking dish with cooking spray.
2. Put the zucchini slices in a colander and sprinkle with salt. Let sit and drain liquid for 5 minutes and pat dry with paper towels. Mix the ricotta, mozzarella, salt, and pepper to evenly combine and spread ¼ cup of the mixture in the bottom of the baking dish.
3. Layer ⅓ of the zucchini slices on top spread 1 cup of tomato sauce over, and scatter a ⅓ cup of spinach on top. Repeat the layering process two more times to exhaust the ingredients while making sure to layer with the last ¼ cup of cheese mixture finally.
4. Grease one end of foil with cooking spray and cover the baking dish with the foil. Bake for 35 minutes, remove foil, and bake further for 5 to 10 minutes or until the cheese has a nice golden brown color. Remove the dish, sit for 5 minutes, make slices of the lasagna, and serve warm.

**Nutrition Info:**

- Info Per Servings 2g Carbs, 7g Protein, 39g Fat, 390 Calories

# Parmesan Roasted Cabbage

Servings: 4

Cooking Time: 25 Minutes

**Ingredients:**

- Cooking spray
- 1 large head green cabbage
- 4 tbsp melted butter
- 1 tsp garlic powder
- Salt and black pepper to taste
- 1 cup grated Parmesan cheese
- Grated Parmesan cheese for topping
- 1 tbsp chopped parsley to garnish

**Directions:**

1. Preheat oven to 400°F, line a baking sheet with foil, and grease with cooking spray.
2. Stand the cabbage and run a knife from the top to bottom to cut the cabbage into wedges. Remove stems and wilted leaves. Mix the butter, garlic, salt, and black pepper until evenly combined.
3. Brush the mixture on all sides of the cabbage wedges and sprinkle with parmesan cheese.
4. Place on the baking sheet, and bake for 20 minutes to soften the cabbage and melt the cheese. Remove the cabbages when golden brown, plate and sprinkle with extra cheese and parsley. Serve warm with pan-glazed tofu.

**Nutrition Info:**

- Info Per Servings 4g Carbs, 17.5g Protein, 19.3g Fat, 268 Calories

# Cauliflower Mac And Cheese

Servings: 7

Cooking Time: 45 Minutes

**Ingredients:**

- 1 cauliflower head, riced
- 1 ½ cups shredded cheese
- 2 tsp paprika
- ¾ tsp rosemary
- 2 tsp turmeric
- 3 eggs

- Olive oil, for frying

**Directions:**

1. Microwave the cauliflower for 5 minutes. Place it in cheesecloth and squeeze the extra juices out. Place the cauliflower in a bowl. Stir in the rest of the ingredients.
2. Heat the oil in a deep pan until it reaches 360°F. Add the 'mac and cheese' and fry until golden and crispy. Drain on paper towels before serving.

**Nutrition Info:**

- Info Per Servings 2g Carbs, 8.6g Protein, 12g Fat, 160 Calories

# Creamy Kale And Mushrooms

Servings: 3

Cooking Time: 15 Minutes

**Ingredients:**

- 3 cloves of garlic, minced
- 1 onion, chopped
- 1 bunch kale, stems removed and leaves chopped
- 3 white button mushrooms, chopped
- 1 cup heavy cream
- 5 tablespoons oil
- Salt and pepper to taste

**Directions:**

1. Heat oil in a pot.
2. Sauté the garlic and onion until fragrant for 2 minutes.
3. Stir in mushrooms. Season with pepper and salt. Cook for 8 minutes.
4. Stir in kale and coconut milk. Simmer for 5 minutes.
5. Adjust seasoning to taste.

**Nutrition Info:**

- Info Per Servings 7.9g Carbs, 6.0g Protein, 35.5g Fat, 365 Calories

# Fish And Seafood Recipes

# Fish And Seafood Recipes

## Halibut With Pesto

Servings: 4

Cooking Time: 15 Minutes

### Ingredients:

- 4 halibut fillets
- 1 cup basil leaves
- 2 cloves of garlic, minced
- 1 tbsp. lemon juice, freshly squeezed
- 2 tbsp pine nuts
- 2 tbsp. oil, preferably extra virgin olive oil
- Salt and pepper to taste

### Directions:

1. In a food processor, pulse the basil, olive oil, pine nuts, garlic, and lemon juice until coarse. Season with salt and pepper to taste.
2. Place a trivet in a large saucepan and pour a cup or two of water into the pan. Bring to a boil.
3. Place salmon in a heatproof dish that fits inside a saucepan. Season salmon with pepper and salt. Drizzle with pesto sauce.
4. Seal dish with foil. Place the dish on the trivet inside the saucepan. Cover and steam for 15 minutes.
5. Serve and enjoy.

### Nutrition Info:

- Info Per Servings 0.8g Carbs, 75.8g Protein, 8.4g Fat, 401 Calories

## Avocado Tuna Boats

Serves: 2

Cooking Time: 10 Minutes

### Ingredients:

- 4 oz tuna, packed in water, drained1 green onion sliced
- 1 avocado, halved, pitted

- 3 tbsp mayonnaise
- 1/3 tsp salt
- Seasoning:
- ¼ tsp ground black pepper
- ¼ tsp paprika

### Directions:

1. Prepare the filling and for this, take a medium bowl, place tuna in it, add green onion, salt, black pepper, paprika and mayonnaise and then stir until well combined.Cut avocado in half lengthwise, then remove the pit and fill with prepared filling. Serve.

### Nutrition Info:

- ; 7 g  Carbs; 8 g Protein; 19 g Fats;  244 Calories

## Enchilada Sauce On Mahi Mahi

Servings: 2

Cooking Time: 15 Minutes

### Ingredients:

- 2 Mahi fillets, fresh
- ¼ cup commercial enchilada sauce
- Pepper to taste

### Directions:

1. In a heat-proof dish that fits inside saucepan, place fish and top with enchilada sauce.
2. Place a large saucepan on the medium-high fire. Place a trivet inside the saucepan and fill the pan halfway with water. Cover and bring to a boil.
3. Cover dish with foil and place on a trivet.
4. Cover pan and steam for 10 minutes. Let it rest in pan for another 5 minutes.
5. Serve and enjoy topped with pepper.

### Nutrition Info:

- Info Per Servings 8.9g Carbs, 19.8g Protein, 15.9g Fat, 257 Calories

# Chipotle Salmon Asparagus

Servings: 2

Cooking Time: 15 Minutes

**Ingredients:**

- 1-lb salmon fillet, skin on
- 2 teaspoon chipotle paste
- A handful of asparagus spears, trimmed
- 1 lemon, sliced thinly
- A pinch of rosemary
- Salt to taste
- 5 tbsp olive oil

**Directions:**

1. In a heat-proof dish that fits inside the saucepan, add asparagus spears on the bottom of the dish. Place fish, top with rosemary, and lemon slices. Season with chipotle paste and salt. Drizzle with olive oil. Cover dish with foil.
2. Place a large saucepan on the medium-high fire. Place a trivet inside the saucepan and fill the pan halfway with water. Cover and bring to a boil.
3. Place dish on the trivet.
4. Cover pan and steam for 10 minutes. Let it rest in pan for another 5 minutes.
5. Serve and enjoy topped with pepper.

**Nutrition Info:**

- Info Per Servings 2.8g Carbs, 35.0g Protein, 50.7g Fat, 651 Calories

# Bang Bang Shrimps

Serves: 2

Cooking Time: 6 Minutes

**Ingredients:**

- 4 oz shrimps¼ tsp paprika
- ¼ tsp apple cider vinegar
- 2 tbsp sweet chili sauce
- ¼ cup mayonnaise
- Seasoning:
- ¼ tsp salt
- 1/8 tsp ground black pepper
- 2 tsp avocado oil

**Directions:**

1. Take a medium skillet pan, place it over medium heat, add oil and wait until it gets hot. Season shrimps with salt, black pepper, and paprika until coated, add them to the pan, and cook for 2 to 3 minutes per side until pink and cooked. Take a medium bowl, place mayonnaise in it, and then whisk in vinegar and chili sauce until combined. Add shrimps into the mayonnaise mixture, toss until coated, and then serve.

**Nutrition Info:**

- 7.2 g Carbs; 13 g Protein; 23.1 g Fats; 290 Calories

# Baked Salmon With Pistachio Crust

Serves:4

Cooking Time: 35 Minutes

**Ingredients:**

- 4 salmon fillets
- ¼ cup mayonnaise
- ½ cup ground pistachios
- 1 chopped shallot
- 2 tsp lemon zest
- 1 tbsp olive oil
- A pinch of pepper
- 1 cup heavy cream

**Directions:**

1. Preheat oven to 375 °F. Brush salmon with mayo and season with salt and pepper. Coat with pistachios. Place in a lined baking dish and bake for 15 minutes. Heat the olive oil in a saucepan and sauté shallot for 3 minutes. Stir in heavy cream and lemon zest. Bring to a boil and cook until thickened. Serve salmon with the sauce.

**Nutrition Info:**

- Per Serves  6g Carbs; 34g Protein; 47g Fat ; 563 Calories

## Steamed Chili-rubbed Tilapia

Servings: 4

Cooking Time: 15 Minutes

**Ingredients:**

- 1 lb. tilapia fillet, skin removed
- 2 tbsp. chili powder
- 3 cloves garlic, peeled and minced
- 2 tbsp. extra virgin olive oil
- 2 tbsp soy sauce

**Directions:**

1. Place a trivet in a large saucepan and pour a cup or two of water into the pan. Bring it to a boil.
2. Place tilapia in a heatproof dish that fits inside a saucepan. Drizzle soy sauce and oil on the filet. Season with chili powder and garlic.
3. Seal dish with foil. Place the dish on the trivet inside the saucepan. Cover and steam for 15 minutes.
4. Serve and enjoy.

**Nutrition Info:**

- Info Per Servings 2g Carbs, 26g Protein, 10g Fat, 211 Calories

## Steamed Herbed Red Snapper

Servings: 4

Cooking Time: 15 Minutes

**Ingredients:**

- 4 red snapper fillets
- ¼ tsp. paprika
- 3 tbsp. lemon juice, freshly squeezed
- 1 ½ tsp chopped fresh herbs of your choice (rosemary, thyme, basil, or parsley)
- 6 tbsp olive oil
- Salt and pepper to taste

**Directions:**

1. In a small bowl, whisk well paprika, lemon juice, olive oil, and herbs. Season with pepper and salt.
2. Place a trivet in a large saucepan and pour a cup

or two of water into the pan. Bring to a boil.
3. Place snapper in a heatproof dish that fits inside a saucepan. Season snapper with pepper and salt. Drizzle with lemon mixture.
4. Seal dish with foil. Place the dish on the trivet inside the saucepan. Cover and steam for 15 minutes.
5. Serve and enjoy.

**Nutrition Info:**

- Info Per Servings 2.1g Carbs, 45.6g Protein, 20.3g Fat, 374 Calories

## Flounder With Dill And Capers

Servings: 4

Cooking Time: 15 Minutes

**Ingredients:**

- 4 flounder fillets
- 1 tbsp. chopped fresh dill
- 2 tbsp. capers, chopped
- 4 lemon wedges
- 6 tbsp olive oil
- Salt and pepper to taste

**Directions:**

1. Place a trivet in a large saucepan and pour a cup or two of water into the pan. Bring to a boil.
2. Place flounder in a heatproof dish that fits inside a saucepan. Season snapper with pepper and salt. Drizzle with olive oil on all sides. Sprinkle dill and capers on top of the filet.
3. Seal dish with foil. Place the dish on the trivet inside the saucepan. Cover and steam for 15 minutes.
4. Serve and enjoy with lemon wedges.

**Nutrition Info:**

- Info Per Servings 8.6g Carbs, 20.3g Protein, 35.9g Fat, 447 Calories

# Grilled Shrimp With Chimichurri Sauce

Servings: 4

Cooking Time: 55 Minutes

**Ingredients:**

- 1 pound shrimp, peeled and deveined
- 2 tbsp olive oil
- Juice of 1 lime
- Chimichurri
- ½ tsp salt
- ¼ cup olive oil
- 2 garlic cloves
- ¼ cup red onion, chopped
- ¼ cup red wine vinegar
- ½ tsp pepper
- 2 cups parsley
- ¼ tsp red pepper flakes

**Directions:**

1. Process the chimichurri ingredients in a blender until smooth; set aside. Combine shrimp, olive oil, and lime juice, in a bowl, and let marinate in the fridge for 30 minutes. Preheat your grill to medium. Add shrimp and cook about 2 minutes per side. Serve shrimp drizzled with the chimichurri sauce.

**Nutrition Info:**

- Info Per Servings 3.5g Carbs, 16g Protein, 20.3g Fat, 283 Calories

## Steamed Asparagus And Shrimps

Servings: 6

Cooking Time: 15 Minutes

**Ingredients:**

- 1-pound shrimps, peeled and deveined
- 1 bunch asparagus, trimmed
- ½ tablespoon Cajun seasoning
- 2 tablespoons butter
- 5 tablespoons oil
- Salt and pepper to taste

**Directions:**

1. In a heat-proof dish that fits inside the saucepan, add all ingredients. Mix well.
2. Place a large saucepan on the medium-high fire. Place a trivet inside the saucepan and fill the pan halfway with water. Cover and bring to a boil.
3. Cover dish with foil and place on a trivet.
4. Cover pan and steam for 10 minutes. Let it rest in pan for another 5 minutes.
5. Serve and enjoy.

**Nutrition Info:**

- Info Per Servings 1.1g Carbs, 15.5g Protein, 15.8g Fat, 204.8 Calories

# Tilapia With Olives & Tomato Sauce

Servings: 4

Cooking Time: 30 Minutes

**Ingredients:**

- 4 tilapia fillets
- 2 garlic cloves, minced
- 2 tsp oregano
- 14 ounces diced tomatoes
- 1 tbsp olive oil
- ½ red onion, chopped
- 2 tbsp parsley
- ¼ cup kalamata olives

**Directions:**

1. Heat the olive oil in a skillet over medium heat and cook the onion for about 3 minutes. Add garlic and oregano and cook for 30 seconds. Stir in tomatoes and bring the mixture to a boil. Reduce the heat and simmer for 5 minutes. Add olives and tilapia, and cook for about 8 minutes. Serve the tilapia with tomato sauce.

**Nutrition Info:**

- Info Per Servings 6g Carbs, 23g Protein, 15g Fat, 282 Calories

# Lemon-rosemary Shrimps

Servings: 4

Cooking Time: 12 Minutes

## Ingredients:

- ½ cup lemon juice, freshly squeezed
- 1 ½ lb. shrimps, peeled and deveined
- 2 tbsp fresh rosemary
- ¼ cup coconut aminos
- 2 tbsp butter
- Pepper to taste
- 4 tbsp olive oil

## Directions:

1. Place a nonstick saucepan on medium-high fire and heat oil and butter for 2 minutes.
2. Stir in shrimps and coconut aminos. Season with pepper. Sauté for 5 minutes.
3. Add remaining ingredients and cook for another 5 minutes while stirring frequently.
4. Serve and enjoy.

## Nutrition Info:

- Info Per Servings 3.7g Carbs, 35.8g Protein, 22.4g Fat, 359 Calories

# Baked Codfish With Lemon

Serves: 4

Cooking Time:25 Minutes

## Ingredients:

- 4 fillets codfish
- 1 teaspoon salt
- 1 teaspoon pepper
- 2 tablespoons olive oil
- 2 teaspoons dried basil
- 2 tablespoons melted butter
- 1 teaspoon dried thyme
- 1/3 teaspoon onion powder
- 2 lemons, juiced
- lemon wedges, for garnish

## Directions:

1. Preheat the oven to 400°F.
2. In a medium bowl combine the lemon juice, onion powder, olive oil, dried basil and thyme. Stir well. Season the fillets with salt and pepper.
3. Top each fillet into the mixture. Then place the fillets into a medium baking dish, greased with melted butter.
4. Bake the codfish fillets for 15-20 minutes. Serve with fresh lemon wedges. Enjoy!

## Nutrition Info:

- Per serving: 3.9g Carbs; 21.2g Protein; 23.6g Fat; 308 Calories

# Salmon Panzanella

Servings: 4

Cooking Time: 22 Minutes

## Ingredients:

- 1 lb skinned salmon, cut into 4 steaks each
- 1 cucumber, peeled, seeded, cubed
- Salt and black pepper to taste
- 8 black olives, pitted and chopped
- 1 tbsp capers, rinsed
- 2 large tomatoes, diced
- 3 tbsp red wine vinegar
- ¼ cup thinly sliced red onion
- 3 tbsp olive oil
- 2 slices day-old zero carb bread, cubed
- ¼ cup thinly sliced basil leaves

## Directions:

1. Preheat a grill to 350ºF and prepare the salad. In a bowl, mix the cucumbers, olives, pepper, capers, tomatoes, wine vinegar, onion, olive oil, bread, and basil leaves. Let sit for the flavors to incorporate.
2. Season the salmon steaks with salt and pepper; grill them on both sides for 8 minutes in total. Serve the salmon steaks warm on a bed of the veggies' salad.

## Nutrition Info:

- Info Per Servings 3.1g Carbs, 28.5g Protein, 21.7g Fat, 338 Calories

# Sautéed Savory Shrimps

Servings: 8

Cooking Time: 15 Minutes

**Ingredients:**

- 2 pounds shrimp, peeled and deveined
- 4 cloves garlic, minced
- ½ cup chicken stock, low sodium
- 1 tablespoon lemon juice
- Salt and pepper
- 5 tablespoons oil

**Directions:**

1. Place a heavy-bottomed pot on medium-high fire and heat pot for 3 minutes.
2. Once hot, add oil and stir around to coat pot with oil.
3. Sauté the garlic and corn for 5 minutes.
4. Add remaining ingredients and mix well.
5. Cover and bring to a boil, lower fire to a simmer, and simmer for 5 minutes.
6. Serve and enjoy.

**Nutrition Info:**

- Info Per Servings 1.7g Carbs, 25.2g Protein, 9.8g Fat, 182.6 Calories

# Avocado & Cauliflower Salad With Prawns

Serves: 6

Cooking Time: 30 Minutes

**Ingredients:**

- 1 cauliflower head, florets only
- 1 lb medium-sized prawns
- ¼ cup + 1 tbsp olive oil
- 1 avocado, chopped
- 3 tbsp chopped dill
- ¼ cup lemon juice
- 2 tbsp lemon zest

**Directions:**

1. Heat 1 tbsp olive oil in a skillet and cook the prawns for 8-10 minutes. Microwave cauliflower for 5 minutes. Place prawns, cauliflower, and avocado in a large bowl. Whisk together the remaining olive oil, lemon zest, juice, dill, and some salt and pepper, in another bowl. Pour the dressing over, toss to combine and serve immediately.

**Nutrition Info:**

- Per Serves  5g Carbs ; 15g Protein ; 17g Fat; 214 Calories

# Cod With Balsamic Tomatoes

Servings: 4

Cooking Time: 30 Minutes

**Ingredients:**

- 4 center-cut bacon strips, chopped
- 4 cod fillets
- 2 cups grape tomatoes, halved
- 2 tablespoons balsamic vinegar
- 4 tablespoons olive oil
- 1/2 teaspoon salt
- 1/4 teaspoon pepper

**Directions:**

1. In a large skillet, heat olive oil and cook bacon over medium heat until crisp, stirring occasionally.
2. Remove with a slotted spoon; drain on paper towels.
3. Sprinkle fillets with salt and pepper. Add fillets to bacon drippings; cook over medium-high heat until fish just begins to flake easily with a fork, 4-6 minutes on each side. Remove and keep warm.
4. Add tomatoes to skillet; cook and stir until tomatoes are softened, 2-4 minutes. Stir in vinegar; reduce heat to medium-low. Cook until sauce is thickened, 1-2 minutes longer.
5. Serve cod with tomato mixture and bacon.

**Nutrition Info:**

- Info Per Servings 5g Carbs, 26g Protein, 30.4g Fat, 442 Calories

# Air Fryer Seasoned Salmon Fillets

Servings: 4

Cooking Time: 10 Mins

**Ingredients:**

- 2 lbs. salmon fillets
- 1 tsp. stevia
- 2 tbsp. whole grain mustard
- 1 clove of garlic, minced
- 1/2 tsp. thyme leaves
- 2 tsp. extra-virgin olive oil
- Cooking spray
- Salt and black pepper to taste

**Directions:**

1. Preheat your Air Fryer to 390 degrees F.
2. Season salmon fillets with salt and pepper.
3. Add together the mustard, garlic, stevia, thyme, and oil in a bowl, stir to combined well. Rub the seasoning mixture on top of salmon fillets.
4. Spray the Air Fryer basket with cooking spray and cook seasoned fillets for 10 minutes until crispy. Let it cool before serving.

**Nutrition Info:**

- Info Per Servings 14g Carbs, 18g Protein, 10g Fat, 238 Calories

# Pistachio-crusted Salmon

Servings: 4

Cooking Time: 35 Minutes

**Ingredients:**

- 4 salmon fillets
- ½ tsp pepper
- 1 tsp salt
- ¼ cup mayonnaise
- ½ cup chopped pistachios
- Sauce
- 1 chopped shallot
- 2 tsp lemon zest
- 1 tbsp olive oil

- A pinch of pepper
- 1 cup heavy cream

**Directions:**

1. Preheat the oven to 370ºF.
2. Brush the salmon with mayonnaise and season with salt and pepper. Coat with pistachios, place in a lined baking dish and bake for 15 minutes.
3. Heat the olive oil in a saucepan and sauté the shallot for 3 minutes. Stir in the rest of the sauce ingredients. Bring the mixture to a boil and cook until thickened. Serve the fish with the sauce.

**Nutrition Info:**

- Info Per Servings 6g Carbs, 34g Protein, 47g Fat, 563 Calories

# Simple Steamed Salmon Fillets

Servings: 3

Cooking Time: 15 Minutes

**Ingredients:**

- 10 oz. salmon fillets
- 2 tbsp. coconut aminos
- 2 tbsp. lemon juice, freshly squeezed
- 1 tsp. sesame seeds, toasted
- 3 tbsp sesame oil
- Salt and pepper to taste

**Directions:**

1. Place a trivet in a large saucepan and pour a cup or two of water into the pan. Bring to a boil.
2. Place salmon in a heatproof dish that fits inside the saucepan. Season salmon with pepper and salt. Drizzle with coconut aminos, lemon juice, sesame oil, and sesame seeds.
3. Seal dish with foil. Place the dish on the trivet inside the saucepan. Cover and steam for 15 minutes.
4. Serve and enjoy.

**Nutrition Info:**

- Info Per Servings 2.6g Carbs, 20.1g Protein, 17.4g Fat, 210 Calories

# Shrimp In Curry Sauce

Servings: 2

Cooking Time: 25 Minutes

**Ingredients:**

- ½ ounces grated Parmesan cheese
- 1 tbsp water
- 1 egg, beaten
- ¼ tsp curry powder
- 2 tsp almond flour
- 12 shrimp, shelled
- 3 tbsp coconut oil
- Sauce
- 2 tbsp curry leaves
- 2 tbsp butter
- ½ onion, diced
- ½ cup heavy cream
- ½ ounce cheddar

**Directions:**

1. Combine all dry ingredients for the batter. Melt the coconut oil in a skillet over medium heat. Dip the shrimp in the egg first, and then coat with the dry mixture. Fry until golden and crispy.
2. In another skillet, melt the butter. Add onion and cook for 3 minutes. Add curry leaves and cook for 30 seconds. Stir in heavy cream and cheddar and cook until thickened. Add the shrimp and coat well. Serve warm.

**Nutrition Info:**

- Info Per Servings 4.3g Carbs, 24.4g Protein, 41g Fat, 560 Calories

# Shrimp And Cauliflower Jambalaya

Servings: 4

Cooking Time: 15 Minutes

**Ingredients:**

- 2 cloves garlic, peeled and minced
- 1 head cauliflower, grated
- 1 cup chopped tomatoes
- 8 oz. raw shrimp, peeled and deveined
- 1 tbsp Cajun seasoning
- Salt and pepper
- 4 tbsp coconut oil
- 1 tbsp water

**Directions:**

1. On medium-high fire, heat a nonstick saucepan for 2 minutes. Add oil to a pan and swirl to coat bottom and sides. Heat oil for a minute.
2. Add garlic and sauté for a minute. Stir in tomatoes and stir fry for 5 minutes. Add water and deglaze the pan.
3. Add remaining ingredients. Season generously with pepper.
4. Increase fire to high and stir fry for 3 minutes.
5. Lower fire to low, cover, and cook for 5 minutes.
6. Serve and enjoy.

**Nutrition Info:**

- Info Per Servings 7.8g Carbs, 21.4g Protein, 22.25g Fat, 314 Calories

# Rosemary-lemon Shrimps

Servings: 4

Cooking Time: 8 Minutes

**Ingredients:**

- 5 tablespoons butter
- ½ cup lemon juice, freshly squeezed
- 1 ½ lb. shrimps, peeled and deveined
- ¼ cup coconut aminos
- 1 tsp rosemary
- Pepper to taste

**Directions:**

1. Place all ingredients in a large pan on a high fire.
2. Boil for 8 minutes or until shrimps are pink.
3. Serve and enjoy.

**Nutrition Info:**

- Info Per Servings 3.7g Carbs, 35.8g Protein, 17.9g Fat, 315 Calories

# Simply Steamed Alaskan Cod

Servings: 2

Cooking Time: 15 Minutes

**Ingredients:**

- 1-lb fillet wild Alaskan Cod
- 1 cup cherry tomatoes, halved
- 1 tbsp balsamic vinegar
- 1 tbsp fresh basil chopped
- Salt and pepper to taste
- 5 tbsp olive oil

**Directions:**

1. In a heat-proof dish that fits inside the saucepan, add all ingredients except for basil. Mix well.
2. Place a large saucepan on the medium-high fire. Place a trivet inside the saucepan and fill pan halfway with water. Cover and bring to a boil.
3. Cover dish with foil and place on a trivet.
4. Cover pan and steam for 10 minutes. Let it rest in pan for another 5 minutes.
5. Serve and enjoy topped with fresh basil.

**Nutrition Info:**

- Info Per Servings 4.2g Carbs, 41.0g Protein, 36.6g Fat, 495.2 Calories

# Salmon And Cauliflower Rice Pilaf

Servings: 4

Cooking Time: 25 Minutes

**Ingredients:**

- 1 cauliflower head, shredded
- ¼ cup dried vegetable soup mix
- 1 cup chicken broth
- 1 pinch saffron
- 1-lb wild salmon fillets
- 6 tbsp olive oil
- Pepper and salt to taste

**Directions:**

1. Place a heavy-bottomed pot on medium-high fire and add all ingredients and mix well.
2. Bring to a boil, lower fire to a simmer, and simmer for 10 minutes.
3. Turn off fire, shred salmon, adjust seasoning to taste.
4. Let it rest for 5 minutes.
5. Fluff again, serve, and enjoy.

**Nutrition Info:**

- Info Per Servings 4.7g Carbs, 31.8g Protein, 31.5g Fat, 429 Calories

# Avocado Salad With Shrimp

Serves: 4

Cooking Time:10 Minutes

**Ingredients:**

- 2 tomatoes, sliced into cubes
- 2 medium avocados, cut into large pieces
- 3 tablespoons red onion, diced
- ½ large lettuce, chopped
- 2 lbs. shrimp, peeled and deveined
- For the Lime Vinaigrette Dressing
- 2 cloves garlic, minced
- 1 ½ teaspoon Dijon mustard
- 1/3 cup extra virgin olive oil
- salt and pepper to taste
- 1/3 cup lime juice

**Directions:**

1. Add the peeled and deveined shrimp and 2 quarts of water to a cooking pot and print to a boil, lower the heat and let them simmer for 1-2 minutes until the shrimp is pink. Set aside and let them cool.
2. Next add the chopped lettuce in a large bowl. Then add the avocado, tomatoes, shrimp and red onion.
3. In a small bowl whisk together the Dijon mustard, garlic, olive oil and lime juice. Mix well.
4. Pour the lime vinaigrette dressing over the salad and serve.

**Nutrition Info:**

- Per serving: 7g Carbs; 43.5g Protein; 17.6g Fat; 377 Calories;

# Golden Pompano In Microwave

Servings: 2

Cooking Time: 11 Minutes

**Ingredients:**

- ½-lb pompano
- 1 tbsp soy sauce, low sodium
- 1-inch thumb ginger, diced
- 1 lemon, halved
- 1 stalk green onions, chopped
- ¼ cup water
- 1 tsp pepper
- 4 tbsp olive oil

**Directions:**

1. In a microwavable casserole dish, mix well all ingredients except for pompano, green onions, and lemon.
2. Squeeze half of the lemon in dish and slice into thin circles the other half.
3. Place pompano in the dish and add lemon circles on top of the fish. Drizzle with pepper and olive oil.
4. Cover top of a casserole dish with a microwave-safe plate.
5. Microwave for 5 minutes.
6. Remove from microwave, turn over fish, sprinkle green onions, top with a microwavable plate.
7. Return to microwave and cook for another 3 minutes.
8. Let it rest for 3 minutes more.
9. Serve and enjoy.

**Nutrition Info:**

- Info Per Servings 6.3g Carbs, 22.2g Protein, 39.5g Fat, 464 Calories

# Baked Calamari And Shrimp

Serves: 1

Cooking Time: 20 Minutes

**Ingredients:**

- 8 ounces calamari, cut in medium rings
- 7 ounces shrimp, peeled and deveined
- 1 eggs
- 3 tablespoons coconut flour
- 1 tablespoon coconut oil
- 2 tablespoons avocado, chopped
- 1 teaspoon tomato paste
- 1 tablespoon mayonnaise
- A splash of Worcestershire sauce
- 1 teaspoon lemon juice
- 2 lemon slices
- Salt and black pepper to the taste
- ½ teaspoon turmeric

**Directions:**

1. In a bowl, whisk egg with coconut oil.
2. Add calamari rings and shrimp and toss to coat.
3. In another bowl, mix flour with salt, pepper and turmeric and stir.
4. Dredge calamari and shrimp in this mix, place everything on a lined baking sheet, introduce in the oven at 400 °F and bake for 10 minutes.
5. Flip calamari and shrimp and bake for 10 minutes more.
6. Meanwhile, in a bowl, mix avocado with mayo and tomato paste and mash using a fork.
7. Add Worcestershire sauce, lemon juice, salt and pepper and stir well.
8. Divide baked calamari and shrimp on plates and serve with the sauce and lemon juice on the side.
9. Enjoy!

**Nutrition Info:**

- 10 carbs; 34 protein; 23 fat; 368 calories

# Sauces And Dressing Recipes

# Sauces And Dressing Recipes

## Keto Ranch Dip

Servings: 8

Cooking Time: 10 Minutes

**Ingredients:**

- 1 cup egg white, beaten
- 1 lemon juice, freshly squeezed
- Salt and pepper to taste
- 1 teaspoon mustard paste
- 1 cup olive oil
- Salt and pepper to taste

**Directions:**

1. Add all ingredients to a pot and bring to a simmer. Stir frequently.
2. Simmer for 10 minutes.
3. Adjust seasoning to taste.

**Nutrition Info:**

- Info Per Servings 1.2g Carbs, 3.4g Protein, 27.1g Fat, 258 Calories

## Ketogenic-friendly Gravy

Servings: 6

Cooking Time: 10 Minutes

**Ingredients:**

- 2 tablespoons butter
- 1 white onion, chopped
- ¼ cup coconut milk
- 2 cups bone broth
- 1 tablespoon balsamic vinegar
- Salt and pepper to taste

**Directions:**

1. Add all ingredients to a pot and bring to a simmer. Stir frequently.
2. Simmer for 10 minutes.

3. Adjust seasoning to taste.

**Nutrition Info:**

- Info Per Servings 1.1g Carbs, 0.2g Protein, 6.3g Fat, 59 Calories

## Vegetarian Fish Sauce

Servings: 16

Cooking Time: 20 Minutes

**Ingredients:**

- 1/4 cup dried shiitake mushrooms
- 1-2 tbsp tamari (for a depth of flavor)
- 3 tbsp coconut aminos
- 1 ¼ cup water
- 2 tsp sea salt

**Directions:**

1. To a small saucepan, add water, coconut aminos, dried shiitake mushrooms, and sea salt. Bring to a boil, then cover, reduce heat, and simmer for 15-20 minutes.
2. Remove from heat and let cool slightly. Pour liquid through a fine-mesh strainer into a bowl, pressing on the mushroom mixture with a spoon to squeeze out any remaining liquid.
3. To the bowl, add tamari. Taste and adjust as needed, adding more sea salt for saltiness.
4. Store in a sealed container in the refrigerator for up to 1 month and shake well before use. Or pour into an ice cube tray, freeze, and store in a freezer-safe container for up to 2 months.

**Nutrition Info:**

- Info Per Servings 5g Carbs, 0.3g Protein, 2g Fat, 39.1 Calories

# Roasted Garlic Lemon Dip

Servings: 3

Cooking Time: 30 Minutes

**Ingredients:**

- 3 medium lemons
- 3 cloves garlic, peeled and smashed
- 5 tablespoons olive oil, divided
- 1/2 teaspoon kosher salt
- Pepper to taste
- Salt
- Pepper

**Directions:**

1. Arrange a rack in the middle of the oven and heat to 400°F.
2. Cut the lemons in half crosswise and remove the seeds. Place the lemons cut-side up in a small baking dish. Add the garlic and drizzle with 2 tablespoons of the oil.
3. Roast until the lemons are tender and lightly browned, about 30 minutes. Remove the baking dish to a wire rack.
4. When the lemons are cool enough to handle, squeeze the juice into the baking dish. Discard the lemon pieces and any remaining seeds. Pour the contents of the baking dish, including the garlic, into a blender or mini food processor. Add the remaining 3 tablespoons oil and salt. Process until the garlic is completely puréed, and the sauce is emulsified and slightly thickened. Serve warm or at room temperature.

**Nutrition Info:**

- Info Per Servings 4.8g Carbs, 0.6g Protein, 17g Fat, 165 Calories

# Dijon Vinaigrette

Servings: 4

Cooking Time: 5 Minutes

**Ingredients:**

- 2 tablespoons Dijon mustard
- Juice of ½ lemon
- 1 garlic clove, finely minced
- 1½ tablespoons red wine vinegar
- Pink Himalayan salt
- Freshly ground black pepper
- 3 tablespoons olive oil

**Directions:**

1. In a small bowl, whisk the mustard, lemon juice, garlic, and red wine vinegar until well combined. Season with pink Himalayan salt and pepper, and whisk again.
2. Slowly add the olive oil, a little bit at a time, whisking constantly.
3. Keep in a sealed glass container in the refrigerator for up to 1 week.

**Nutrition Info:**

- Info Per Servings 1g Carbs, 1g Protein, 11g Fat, 99 Calories

# Avocado-lime Crema

Servings: 4

Cooking Time: 5 Minutes

**Ingredients:**

- ½ cup sour cream
- ½ avocado
- 1 garlic clove, finely minced
- ¼ cup fresh cilantro leaves
- Juice of ½ lime
- Pinch pink Himalayan salt
- Pinch freshly ground black pepper

**Directions:**

1. In a food processor (or blender), mix the sour cream, avocado, garlic, cilantro, lime juice, pink Himalayan salt, and pepper until smooth and fully combined.
2. Spoon the sauce into an airtight glass jar and keep in the refrigerator for up to 3 days.

**Nutrition Info:**

- Info Per Servings Calories: 2g Carbs, 1g Protein, 8g Fat, 87 Calories

# Caesar Dressing

Servings: 4

Cooking Time: 5 Minutes

**Ingredients:**

- ½ cup mayonnaise
- 1 tablespoon Dijon mustard
- Juice of ½ lemon
- ½ teaspoon Worcestershire sauce
- Pinch pink Himalayan salt
- Pinch freshly ground black pepper
- ¼ cup grated Parmesan cheese

**Directions:**

1. In a medium bowl, whisk together the mayonnaise, mustard, lemon juice, Worcestershire sauce, pink Himalayan salt, and pepper until fully combined.
2. Add the Parmesan cheese, and whisk until creamy and well blended.
3. Keep in a sealed glass container in the refrigerator for up to 1 week.

**Nutrition Info:**

- Info Per Servings Calories: 2g Carbs, 2g Protein, 23g Fat, 222 Calories

# Keto Thousand Island Dressing

Servings: 10

Cooking Time: 10 Minutes

**Ingredients:**

- 1 cup mayonnaise
- 1 tablespoon lemon juice, freshly squeezed
- 4 tablespoons dill pickles, chopped
- 1 teaspoon Tabasco
- 1 shallot chopped finely
- Salt and pepper to taste

**Directions:**

1. Add all ingredients to a pot and bring to a simmer. Stir frequently.
2. Simmer for 10 minutes.

3. Adjust seasoning to taste.

**Nutrition Info:**

- Info Per Servings 2.3g Carbs, 1.7g Protein, 7.8g Fat, 85 Calories

# Tzatziki

Servings: 4

Cooking Time: 10 Minutes, Plus At Least 30 Minutes To Chill

**Ingredients:**

- ½ large English cucumber, unpeeled
- 1½ cups Greek yogurt (I use Fage)
- 2 tablespoons olive oil
- Large pinch pink Himalayan salt
- Large pinch freshly ground black pepper
- Juice of ½ lemon
- 2 garlic cloves, finely minced
- 1 tablespoon fresh dill

**Directions:**

1. Halve the cucumber lengthwise, and use a spoon to scoop out and discard the seeds.
2. Grate the cucumber with a zester or grater onto a large plate lined with a few layers of paper towels. Close the paper towels around the grated cucumber, and squeeze as much water out of it as you can. (This can take a while and can require multiple paper towels. You can also allow it to drain overnight in a strainer or wrapped in a few layers of cheesecloth in the fridge if you have the time.)
3. In a food processor (or blender), blend the yogurt, olive oil, pink Himalayan salt, pepper, lemon juice, and garlic until fully combined.
4. Transfer the mixture to a medium bowl, and mix in the fresh dill and grated cucumber.
5. I like to chill this sauce for at least 30 minutes before serving. Keep in a sealed glass container in the refrigerator for up to 1 week.

**Nutrition Info:**

- Info Per Servings 5g Carbs, 8g Protein, 11g Fat, 149 Calories

# Cheesy Avocado Dip

Servings:

Cooking Time: 20 Minutes

**Ingredients:**

- 1/2 medium ripe avocado, peeled and pitted
- 2 crumbled blue cheese
- 1 freshly squeezed lemon juice
- 1/2 kosher salt
- 1/2 cup water

**Directions:**

1. Scoop the flesh of the avocado into the bowl of a food processor fitted with the blade attachment or blender.
2. Add the blue cheese, lemon juice, and salt. Blend until smooth and creamy, 30 to 40 seconds.
3. With the motor running, add the water and blend until the sauce is thinned and well-combined.

**Nutrition Info:**

- Info Per Servings 2.9g Carbs, 3.5g Protein, 7.2g Fat, 86 Calories

# Caesar Salad Dressing

Servings: 6

Cooking Time: 10 Minutes

**Ingredients:**

- ½ cup olive oil
- 1 tablespoon Dijon mustard
- ½ cup parmesan cheese, grated
- 2/3-ounce anchovies, chopped
- ½ lemon juice, freshly squeezed
- Salt and pepper to taste

**Directions:**

1. Add all ingredients to a pot and bring to a simmer. Stir frequently.
2. Simmer for 10 minutes.
3. Adjust seasoning to taste.

**Nutrition Info:**

- Info Per Servings 1.5g Carbs, 3.4g Protein, 20.7g Fat, 203 Calories

# Alfredo Sauce

Servings: 2

Cooking Time: 10 Minutes

**Ingredients:**

- 4 tablespoons butter
- 2 ounces cream cheese
- 1 cup heavy (whipping) cream
- ½ cup grated Parmesan cheese
- 1 garlic clove, finely minced
- 1 teaspoon dried Italian seasoning
- Pink Himalayan salt
- Freshly ground black pepper

**Directions:**

1. In a heavy medium saucepan over medium heat, combine the butter, cream cheese, and heavy cream. Whisk slowly and constantly until the butter and cream cheese melt.
2. Add the Parmesan, garlic, and Italian seasoning. Continue to whisk until everything is well blended. Turn the heat to medium-low and simmer, stirring occasionally, for 5 to 8 minutes to allow the sauce to blend and thicken.
3. Season with pink Himalayan salt and pepper, and stir to combine.
4. Toss with your favorite hot, precooked, keto-friendly noodles and serve.
5. Keep this sauce in a sealed glass container in the refrigerator for up to 4 days.

**Nutrition Info:**

- Info Per Servings 2g Carbs, 5g Protein, 30g Fat, 294 Calories

# Green Jalapeno Sauce

Servings: 1

Cooking Time: 0 Minutes

**Ingredients:**

- ½ avocado
- 1 large jalapeno
- 1 cup fresh cilantro
- 2 tablespoons extra virgin olive oil
- 3 tablespoons water
- Water
- ½ teaspoon salt

**Directions:**

1. Add all ingredients in a blender.
2. Blend until smooth and creamy.
3. Serve and enjoy.

**Nutrition Info:**

- Info Per Servings 10g Carbs, 2.4g Protein, 42g Fat, 407 Calories

# Celery-onion Vinaigrette

Servings: 4

Cooking Time: 0 Minutes

**Ingredients:**

- 1 tbsp finely chopped celery
- 1 tbsp finely chopped red onion
- 4 garlic cloves, minced
- ½ cup red wine vinegar
- 1 tbsp extra virgin olive oil

**Directions:**

1. Prepare the dressing by mixing pepper, celery, onion, olive oil, garlic, and vinegar in a small bowl. Whisk well to combine.
2. Let it sit for at least 30 minutes to let flavors blend.
3. Serve and enjoy with your favorite salad greens.

**Nutrition Info:**

- Info Per Servings 1.4g Carbs, 0.2g Protein, 3.4g

Fat, 41 Calories

# Garlic Aioli

Servings: 4

Cooking Time: 5 Minutes, Plus 30 Minutes To Chill

**Ingredients:**

- ½ cup mayonnaise
- 2 garlic cloves, minced
- Juice of 1 lemon
- 1 tablespoon chopped fresh flat-leaf Italian parsley
- 1 teaspoon chopped chives
- Pink Himalayan salt
- Freshly ground black pepper

**Directions:**

1. In a food processor (or blender), combine the mayonnaise, garlic, lemon juice, parsley, and chives, and season with pink Himalayan salt and pepper. Blend until fully combined.
2. Pour into a sealed glass container and chill in the refrigerator for at least 30 minutes before serving. (This sauce will keep in the fridge for up to 1 week.)

**Nutrition Info:**

- Info Per Servings Calories: 3g Carbs, 1g Protein, 22g Fat, 204 Calories

# Peanut Sauce

Servings: 4

Cooking Time: 5 Minutes

**Ingredients:**

- ½ cup creamy peanut butter (I use Justin's)
- 2 tablespoons soy sauce (or coconut aminos)
- 1 teaspoon Sriracha sauce
- 1 teaspoon toasted sesame oil
- 1 teaspoon garlic powder

**Directions:**

1. In a food processor (or blender), blend the peanut butter, soy sauce, Sriracha sauce, sesame oil, and garlic powder until thoroughly mixed.
2. Pour into an airtight glass container and keep in the refrigerator for up to 1 week.

**Nutrition Info:**

- Info Per Servings Calories: 185; Total Fat: 15g; Carbs: 8g; Net Carbs: 6g; Fiber: 2g; Protein: 7g

# Artichoke Pesto Dip

Servings: 1

Cooking Time: 20 Minutes

**Ingredients:**

- 1 jar marinated artichoke hearts
- 8 ounces cream cheese (at room temperature)
- 4 ounces parmesan cheese (grated)
- 2 tablespoons basil pesto
- ¼ cup shelled pistachio (chopped, optional)

**Directions:**

1. Preheat oven to 375oF.
2. Drain and chop artichoke hearts.
3. Mix artichokes, cream cheese, parmesan, and pesto.
4. Pour into 4 ramekins evenly.
5. Bake for 15-20 minutes.

**Nutrition Info:**

- Info Per Servings 5g Carbs, 8g Protein, 19g Fat,

214 Calories

# Simple Tomato Sauce

Servings: 4

Cooking Time: 20 Minutes

**Ingredients:**

- 1 can whole peeled tomatoes
- 3 garlic cloves, smashed
- 5 tablespoons olive oil
- Kosher salt
- 2 tablespoons unsalted butter
- Salt

**Directions:**

1. Purée tomatoes in a food processor until they're as smooth or chunky as you like.
2. Transfer tomatoes to a large Dutch oven or other heavy pot. (Or, use an immersion blender and blend directly in the pot.)
3. Add garlic, oil, and a 5-finger pinch of salt.
4. Bring to a boil and cook, occasionally stirring, until sauce is reduced by about one-third, about 20 minutes. Stir in butter.

**Nutrition Info:**

- Info Per Servings 7.6g Carbs, 1.9g Protein, 21.3g Fat, 219 Calories

# Fat-burning Dressing

Servings: 6

Cooking Time: 3 Minutes

**Ingredients:**

- 2 tablespoons coconut oil
- ¼ cup olive oil
- 2 cloves of garlic, minced
- 2 tablespoons freshly chopped herbs of your choice
- ¼ cup mayonnaise
- Salt and pepper to taste

**Directions:**

1. Heat the coconut oil and olive oil and sauté the garlic until fragrant in a saucepan.
2. Allow cooling slightly before adding the mayonnaise.
3. Season with salt and pepper to taste.

**Nutrition Info:**

- Info Per Servings 0.6g Carbs, 14.1g Protein, 22.5g Fat, 262 Calories

# Green Goddess Dressing

Servings: 4

Cooking Time: 5 Minutes

**Ingredients:**

- 2 tablespoon buttermilk
- ¼ cup Greek yogurt
- 1 teaspoon apple cider vinegar
- 1 garlic clove, minced
- 1 tablespoon olive oil
- 1 tablespoon fresh parsley leaves

**Directions:**

1. In a food processor (or blender), combine the buttermilk, yogurt, apple cider vinegar, garlic, olive oil, and parsley. Blend until fully combined.
2. Pour into a sealed glass container and chill in the refrigerator for at least 30 minutes before serving. This dressing will keep in the fridge for up to 1 week.

**Nutrition Info:**

- Info Per Servings 1g Carbs, 1g Protein, 6g Fat, 62 Calories

# Lemon Tahini Sauce

Servings: 2

Cooking Time: 5 Minutes

**Ingredients:**

- 1/2 cup packed fresh herbs, such as parsley, basil, mint, cilantro, dill, or chives
- 1/4 cup tahini
- Juice of 1 lemon
- 1/2 teaspoon kosher salt
- 1 tablespoon water

**Directions:**

1. Place all the ingredients in the bowl of a food processor fitted with the blade attachment or a blender. Process continuously until the herbs are finely minced, and the sauce is well-blended, 3 to 4 minutes.
2. Serve immediately or store in a covered container in the refrigerator until ready to serve.

**Nutrition Info:**

- Info Per Servings 4.3g Carbs, 2.8g Protein, 8.1g Fat, 94 Calories

# Buttery Dijon Sauce

Servings: 2

Cooking Time: 0 Minutes

## Ingredients:

- 3 parts brown butter
- 1-part vinegar or citrus juice or a combo
- 1-part strong Dijon mustard
- A small handful of flat-leaf parsley (optional)
- 3/4 teaspoon freshly ground pepper
- 1 teaspoon salt

## Directions:

1. Add everything to a food processor and blitz until just smooth.
2. You can also mix this up with an immersion blender. Use immediately or store in the refrigerator for up to one day. Blend again before use.

## Nutrition Info:

- Info Per Servings 0.7g Carbs, 0.4g Protein, 34.4g Fat, 306 Calories

# Buffalo Sauce

Servings: 8

Cooking Time: 30 Minutes

## Ingredients:

- 8 ounces Cream Cheese (softened)
- ½ cup Buffalo Wing Sauce
- ½ cup Blue Cheese Dressing
- 1 ½ cups Cheddar Cheese (Shredded)
- 1 ¼ cups Chicken Breast (Cooked)

## Directions:

1. Preheat oven to 350oF.
2. Blend together buffalo sauce, white salad dressing, cream cheese, chicken, and shredded cheese.
3. Top with any other optional ingredients like blue cheese chunks.
4. Bake for 25-30 minutes

## Nutrition Info:

- Info Per Servings 2.2g Carbs, 16g Protein, 28g Fat, 325 Calories

# Avocado Mayo

Servings: 4

Cooking Time: 5 Minutes

## Ingredients:

- 1 medium avocado, cut into chunks
- ½ teaspoon ground cayenne pepper
- Juice of ½ lime
- 2 tablespoons fresh cilantro leaves (optional)
- Pinch pink Himalayan salt
- ¼ cup olive oil

## Directions:

1. In a food processor (or blender), blend the avocado, cayenne pepper, lime juice, cilantro, and pink Himalayan salt until all the ingredients are well combined and smooth.
2. Slowly incorporate the olive oil, adding 1 tablespoon at a time, pulsing the food processor in between.
3. Keep in a sealed glass container in the refrigerator for up to 1 week.

## Nutrition Info:

- Info Per Servings 1g Carbs, 1g Protein, 5g Fat, 58 Calories

# Desserts And Drinks

# Desserts And Drinks

## Brownies With Coco Milk

Servings: 10

Cooking Time: 6 Hours

**Ingredients:**

- ¾ cup coconut milk
- 1 teaspoon erythritol
- 2 tablespoons butter, melted
- 4 egg yolks, beaten
- 5 tablespoons cacao powder

**Directions:**

1. In a bowl, mix well all ingredients.
2. Lightly grease your slow cooker with cooking spray and pour in batter.
3. Cover and cook on low for six hours.
4. Serve and enjoy.

**Nutrition Info:**

- Info Per Servings 1.2g Carbs, 1.5g Protein, 8.4g Fat, 86 Calories

## Almond Milk Hot Chocolate

Servings: 4

Cooking Time: 7 Minutes

**Ingredients:**

- 3 cups almond milk
- 4 tbsp unsweetened cocoa powder
- 2 tbsp swerve
- 3 tbsp almond butter
- Finely chopped almonds to garnish

**Directions:**

1. In a saucepan, add the almond milk, cocoa powder, and swerve. Stir the mixture until the sugar dissolves. Set the pan over low to heat through for 5 minutes, without boiling.

2. Swirl the mix occasionally. Turn the heat off and stir in the almond butter to be incorporated. Pour the hot chocolate into mugs and sprinkle with chopped almonds. Serve warm.

**Nutrition Info:**

- Info Per Servings 0.6g Carbs, 4.5g Protein, 21.5g Fat, 225 Calories

## Fast 'n Easy Cookie In A Mug

Servings: 1

Cooking Time: 5 Minutes

**Ingredients:**

- 1 tablespoon butter
- 3 tablespoons almond flour
- 1 tablespoon erythritol
- 1 egg yolk
- 1/8 teaspoon vanilla extract
- A dash of cinnamon
- A pinch of salt

**Directions:**

1. Mix all ingredients in a microwave-safe mug.
2. Nuke in the microwave for 3 minutes.
3. Let it rest for a minute.
4. Serve and enjoy.

**Nutrition Info:**

- Info Per Servings 1.4g Carbs, 3.5g Protein, 17.8g Fat, 180 Calories

# Spicy Cheese Crackers

Servings: 4

Cooking Time: 10 Mins

**Ingredients:**

- 3/4 cup almond flour
- 1 egg
- 2 tablespoons cream cheese
- 2 cups shredded Parmesan cheese
- 1/2 teaspoon red pepper flakes
- 1 tablespoon dry ranch salad dressing mix

**Directions:**

1. Preheat oven to 425 degrees F.
2. Combine Parmesan and cream cheese in a microwave safe bowl and microwave in 30 second intervals. Add the cheese to mix well, and whisk along the almond flour, egg, ranch seasoning, and red pepper flakes, stirring occasionally.
3. Transfer the dough in between two parchment-lined baking sheets. Form the dough into rolls by cutting off plum-sized pieces of dough with dough cutter into 1-inch square pieces, yielding about 60 pieces.
4. Place crackers to a baking sheet lined parchment. Bake for 5 minutes, flipping halfway, then continue to bake for 5 minutes more. Chill before serving.

**Nutrition Info:**

- Info Per Servings 18g Carbs, 17g Protein, 4g Fat, 235 Calories

# Mint Chocolate Protein Shake

Servings: 4

Cooking Time: 4 Minutes

**Ingredients:**

- 3 cups flax milk, chilled
- 3 tsp unsweetened cocoa powder
- 1 avocado, pitted, peeled, sliced
- 1 cup coconut milk, chilled
- 3 mint leaves + extra to garnish
- 3 tbsp erythritol

- 1 tbsp low carb Protein powder
- Whipping cream for topping

**Directions:**

1. Combine the milk, cocoa powder, avocado, coconut milk, mint leaves, erythritol, and protein powder into a blender, and blend for 1 minute until smooth.
2. Pour into serving glasses, lightly add some whipping cream on top, and garnish with mint leaves.

**Nutrition Info:**

- Info Per Servings 4g Carbs, 15g Protein, 14.5g Fat, 191 Calories

# Walnut Cookies

Servings: 12

Cooking Time: 25 Minutes

**Ingredients:**

- 1 egg
- 2 cups ground pecans
- ¼ cup sweetener
- ½ tsp baking soda
- 1 tbsp butter
- 20 walnuts halves

**Directions:**

1. Preheat the oven to 350ºF. Mix the ingredients, except the walnuts, until combined. Make 20 balls out of the mixture and press them with your thumb onto a lined cookie sheet. Top each cookie with a walnut half. Bake for about 12 minutes.

**Nutrition Info:**

- Info Per Servings 0.6g Carbs, 1.6g Protein, 11g Fat, 101 Calories

# Green And Fruity Smoothie

Servings: 2

Cooking Time: 0 Minutes

**Ingredients:**

- 1 cup spinach, packed
- ½ cup strawberries, chopped
- ½ avocado, peeled, pitted, and frozen
- 1 tbsp almond butter
- ¼ cup packed kale, stem discarded, and leaves chopped
- 1 cup ice-cold water
- 5 tablespoons MCT oil or coconut oil

**Directions:**

1. Blend all ingredients in a blender until smooth and creamy.
2. Serve and enjoy.

**Nutrition Info:**

- Info Per Servings 10g Carbs, 1.6g Protein, 47.3g Fat, 459 Calories

# Coconut-mocha Shake

Servings: 1

Cooking Time: 0 Minutes

**Ingredients:**

- 2 tbsp cocoa powder
- 1 tbsp coconut flakes, unsweetened
- 2 packet Stevia, or more to taste
- 1 cup brewed coffee, chilled
- 3 tbsps coconut oil

**Directions:**

1. Add all ingredients in a blender.
2. Blend until smooth and creamy.
3. Serve and enjoy.

**Nutrition Info:**

- Info Per Servings 9g Carbs, 2.4g Protein, 43.7g Fat, 402 Calories

# Nutty Greens Shake

Servings: 1

Cooking Time: 0 Minutes

**Ingredients:**

- ½ cup half and half, liquid
- 1 packet Stevia, or more to taste
- 3 pecan nuts
- 3 macadamia nuts
- 1 cup spring mix salad greens
- 1 ½ cups water
- 3 tablespoons coconut oil

**Directions:**

1. Add all ingredients in a blender.
2. Blend until smooth and creamy.
3. Serve and enjoy.

**Nutrition Info:**

- Info Per Servings 10.5g Carbs, 7.0g Protein, 65.6g Fat, 628 Calories

# Choco Coffee Milk Shake

Servings: 1

Cooking Time: 0 Minutes

**Ingredients:**

- ½ cup coconut milk
- 1 tbsp cocoa powder
- 1 cup brewed coffee, chilled
- 1 packet Stevia, or more to taste
- ½ tsp cinnamon
- 5 tbsps coconut oil

**Directions:**

1. Add all ingredients in a blender.
2. Blend until smooth and creamy.
3. Serve and enjoy.

**Nutrition Info:**

- Info Per Servings 10g Carbs, 4.1g Protein, 97.4g Fat, 880 Calories

# Nutty Choco Milk Shake

Servings: 1

Cooking Time: 0 Minutes

**Ingredients:**

- ¼ cup half and half
- 1 tbsp cocoa powder
- 1 packet Stevia, or more to taste
- 4 pecans
- 1 tbsp macadamia oil
- 1 ½ cups water
- 3 tbsp coconut oil

**Directions:**

1. Add all ingredients in a blender.
2. Blend until smooth and creamy.
3. Serve and enjoy.

**Nutrition Info:**

- Info Per Servings 9.4g Carbs, 4.8g Protein, 73g Fat, 689 Calories

# No Nuts Fudge

Servings: 15

Cooking Time: 4 Hours

**Ingredients:**

- ¼ cup cocoa powder
- ½ teaspoon baking powder
- 1 stick of butter, melted
- 4 tablespoons erythritol
- 6 eggs, beaten
- Salt to taste.

**Directions:**

1. Mix all ingredients in a slow cooker.
2. Add a pinch of salt.
3. Mix until well combined.
4. Cover pot.
5. Press the low settings and adjust the time to 4 hours.

**Nutrition Info:**

- Info Per Servings 1.3g Carbs, 4.3g Protein, 12.2g Fat, 132 Calories

# Cranberry White Chocolate Barks

Servings: 6

Cooking Time: 5 Minutes

**Ingredients:**

- 10 oz unsweetened white chocolate, chopped
- ½ cup erythritol
- ⅓ cup dried cranberries, chopped
- ⅓ cup toasted walnuts, chopped
- ¼ tsp pink salt

**Directions:**

1. Line a baking sheet with parchment paper. Pour chocolate and erythritol in a bowl, and melt in the microwave for 25 seconds, stirring three times until fully melted. Stir in the cranberries, walnuts, and salt, reserving a few cranberries and walnuts for garnishing.
2. Pour the mixture on the baking sheet and spread out. Sprinkle with remaining cranberries and walnuts. Refrigerate for 2 hours to set. Break into bite-size pieces to serve.

**Nutrition Info:**

- Info Per Servings 3g Carbs, 6g Protein, 21g Fat, 225 Calories

# Lemon Cheesecake Mousse

Servings: 4

Cooking Time: 5 Minutes +cooling Time

**Ingredients:**

- 24 oz cream cheese, softened
- 2 cups swerve confectioner's sugar
- 2 lemons, juiced and zested
- Pink salt to taste
- 1 cup whipped cream + extra for garnish

**Directions:**

1. Whip the cream cheese in a bowl with a hand mixer until light and fluffy. Mix in the sugar, lemon juice, and salt. Fold in the whipped cream to evenly combine.
2. Spoon the mousse into serving cups and refrigerate to thicken for 1 hour. Swirl with extra whipped cream and garnish lightly with lemon zest. Serve immediately.

**Nutrition Info:**

- Info Per Servings 3g Carbs, 12g Protein, 18g Fat, 223 Calories

# Nutritiously Green Milk Shake

Servings: 1

Cooking Time: 5 Minutes

**Ingredients:**

- 1 cup coconut cream
- 1 packet Stevia, or more to taste
- 1 tbsp coconut flakes, unsweetened
- 2 cups spring mix salad
- 3 tbsps coconut oil
- 1 cup water

**Directions:**

1. Add all ingredients in a blender.
2. Blend until smooth and creamy.
3. Serve and enjoy.

**Nutrition Info:**

- Info Per Servings 10g Carbs, 10.5g Protein, 95.3g Fat, 887 Calories

# Cinnamon Cookies

Servings: 4

Cooking Time: 25 Minutes

**Ingredients:**

- 2 cups almond flour
- ½ tsp baking soda
- ¾ cup sweetener
- ½ cup butter, softened
- A pinch of salt
- Coating:
- 2 tbsp erythritol sweetener
- 1 tsp cinnamon

**Directions:**

1. Preheat your oven to 350°F. Combine all cookie ingredients in a bowl. Make 16 balls out of the mixture and flatten them with hands. Combine the cinnamon and erythritol. Dip the cookies in the cinnamon mixture and arrange them on a lined cookie sheet. Cook for 15 minutes, until crispy.

**Nutrition Info:**

- Info Per Servings 1.5g Carbs, 3g Protein, 13g Fat, 131 Calories

# Passion Fruit Cheesecake Slices

Servings: 8

Cooking Time: 2 Hours 30 Minutes

**Ingredients:**

- 1 cup crushed almond biscuits
- ½ cup melted butter
- Filling:
- 1 ½ cups cream cheese
- ¾ cup swerve
- 1 ½ whipping cream
- 1 tsp vanilla bean paste
- 4-6 tbsp cold water
- 1 tbsp gelatin powder
- Passionfruit Jelly
- 1 cup passion fruit pulp
- ¼ cup swerve confectioner's sugar
- 1 tsp gelatin powder
- ¼ cup water, room temperature

**Directions:**

1. Mix the crushed biscuits and butter in a bowl, spoon into a spring-form pan, and use the back of the spoon to level at the bottom. Set aside in the fridge. Put the cream cheese, swerve, and vanilla paste into a bowl, and use the hand mixer to whisk until smooth; set aside.
2. In a bowl, add 2 tbsp of cold water and sprinkle 1 tbsp of gelatin powder. Let dissolve for 5 minutes. Pour the gelatin liquid along with the whipping cream in the cheese mixture and fold gently.
3. Remove the spring-form pan from the refrigerator and pour over the mixture. Return to the fridge.
4. Repeat the dissolving process for the remaining gelatin and once your out of ingredients, pour the confectioner's sugar, and ¼ cup of water into it. Mix and stir in the passion fruit pulp.
5. Remove the cake again and pour the jelly over it. Swirl the pan to make the jelly level up. Place the pan back into the fridge to cool for 2 hours. When completely set, remove and unlock the spring-pan. Lift the pan from the cake and slice the dessert.

**Nutrition Info:**

- Info Per Servings 6.1g Carbs, 4.4g Protein, 18g Fat, 287 Calories

# Raspberry Sorbet

Servings: 1

Cooking Time: 3 Minutes

**Ingredients:**

- ¼ tsp vanilla extract
- 1 packet gelatine, without sugar
- 1 tbsp heavy whipping cream
- ⅓ cup boiling water
- 2 tbsp mashed raspberries
- 1 ½ cups crushed Ice
- ⅓ cup cold water

**Directions:**

1. Combine the gelatin and boiling water, until completely dissolved; then transfer to a blender. Add the remaining ingredients. Blend until smooth and freeze for at least 2 hours.

**Nutrition Info:**

- Info Per Servings 3.7g Carbs, 4g Protein, 10g Fat, 173 Calories

# Almond Choco Shake

Servings: 1

Cooking Time: 0 Minutes

**Ingredients:**

- ½ cup heavy cream, liquid
- 1 tbsp cocoa powder
- 1 packet Stevia, or more to taste
- 5 almonds, chopped
- 1 ½ cups water
- 3 tbsp coconut oil

**Directions:**

1. Add all ingredients in a blender.
2. Blend until smooth and creamy.
3. Serve and enjoy.

**Nutrition Info:**

- Info Per Servings 9.7g Carbs, 11.9g Protein, 45.9g Fat, 485 Calories

# White Chocolate Cheesecake Bites

Servings: 12

Cooking Time: 4 Minutes + Cooling Time

**Ingredients:**

- 10 oz unsweetened white chocolate chips
- ½ half and half
- 20 oz cream cheese, softened
- ½ cup swerve
- 1 tsp vanilla extract

**Directions:**

1. In a saucepan, melt the chocolate with half and a half on low heat for 1 minute. Turn the heat off.
2. In a bowl, whisk the cream cheese, swerve, and vanilla extract with a hand mixer until smooth. Stir into the chocolate mixture. Spoon into silicone muffin tins and freeze for 4 hours until firm.

**Nutrition Info:**

- Info Per Servings 3.1g Carbs, 5g Protein, 22g Fat, 241 Calories

# Lettuce Green Shake

Servings: 1

Cooking Time: 0 Minutes

**Ingredients:**

- ¾ cup whole milk yogurt
- 2 cups 5-lettuce mix salad greens
- 3 tbsp MCT oil
- 1 tbsp chia seeds
- 1 ½ cups water
- 1 packet Stevia, or more to taste

**Directions:**

1. Add all ingredients in a blender.
2. Blend until smooth and creamy.
3. Serve and enjoy.

**Nutrition Info:**

- Info Per Servings 6.1g Carbs, 8.1g Protein, 47g Fat, 483 Calories

# Ice Cream Bars Covered With Chocolate

Servings: 15

Cooking Time: 4 Hours And 20 Minutes

**Ingredients:**

- Ice Cream:
- 1 cup heavy whipping cream
- 1 tsp vanilla extract
- ¾ tsp xanthan gum
- ½ cup peanut butter
- 1 cup half and half
- 1 ½ cups almond milk
- ⅓ tsp stevia powder
- 1 tbsp vegetable glycerin
- 3 tbsp xylitol
- Chocolate:
- ¾ cup coconut oil
- ¼ cup cocoa butter pieces, chopped
- 2 ounces unsweetened chocolate
- 3 ½ tsp THM super sweet blend

**Directions:**

1. Blend all ice cream ingredients until smooth. Place in an ice cream maker and follow the instructions. Spread the ice cream into a lined pan, and freezer for about 4 hours.
2. Combine all chocolate ingredients in a microwave-safe bowl and heat until melted. Allow cooling. Remove the ice cream from the freezer and slice into bars. Dip them into the cooled chocolate mixture and return to the freezer for about 10 minutes before serving.

**Nutrition Info:**

- Info Per Servings 5g Carbs, 4g Protein, 32g Fat, 345 Calories

# White Choco Fatty Fudge

Servings: 6

Cooking Time: 10 Minutes

**Ingredients:**

- 1/4 cup coconut butter
- 1/4 cup cashew butter
- 2 tbsp cacao butter
- 1/4 teaspoon vanilla powder
- 10–12 drops liquid stevia, or to taste
- 2 tbsp coconut oil

**Directions:**

1. Over low heat, place a small saucepan and melt coconut oil, cacao butter, cashew butter, and coconut butter.
2. Remove from the heat and stir in the vanilla and stevia.
3. Pour into a silicone mold and place it in the freezer for 30 minutes.
4. Store in the fridge for a softer consistency.

**Nutrition Info:**

- Info Per Servings 1.7g Carbs, 0.2g Protein, 23.7g Fat, 221 Calories

# Chocolate Chip Cookies

Servings: 4

Cooking Time: 20 Minutes

**Ingredients:**

- 1 cup butter, softened
- 2 cups swerve brown sugar
- 3 eggs
- 2 cups almond flour
- 2 cups unsweetened chocolate chips

**Directions:**

1. Preheat oven to 350ºF and line a baking sheet with parchment paper.
2. Whisk the butter and sugar with a hand mixer for 3 minutes or until light and fluffy. Add the eggs one at a time, and scrape the sides as you whisk.

Mix in the almond flour in low speed until well combined.
3. Fold in the chocolate chips. Scoop 3 tablespoons each on the baking sheet creating spaces between each mound and bake for 15 minutes to swell and harden. Remove, cool and serve.

**Nutrition Info:**

- Info Per Servings 8.9g Carbs, 6.3g Protein, 27g Fat, 317 Calories

# Cardamom-cinnamon Spiced Co-co-latte

Servings: 1

Cooking Time: 0 Minutes

**Ingredients:**

- ½ cup coconut milk
- ¼ tsp cardamom powder
- 1 tbsp chocolate powder
- 1 ½ cups brewed coffee, chilled
- 1 tbsp coconut oil
- ¼ tsp cinnamon
- ¼ tsp nutmeg

**Directions:**

1. Add all ingredients in a blender.
2. Blend until smooth and creamy.
3. Serve and enjoy.

**Nutrition Info:**

- Info Per Servings 7.5g Carbs, 3.8g Protein, 38.7g Fat, 362 Calories

# Vanilla Flan With Mint

Servings: 4

Cooking Time: 10 Minutes

**Ingredients:**

- ⅓ cup erythritol, for caramel
- 2 cups almond milk
- 4 eggs
- 1 tbsp vanilla
- 1 tbsp lemon zest
- ½ cup erythritol, for custard
- 2 cup heavy whipping cream
- Mint leaves, to serve

**Directions:**

1. Heat the erythritol for the caramel in a deep pan. Add 2-3 tablespoons of water, and bring to a boil. Reduce the heat and cook until the caramel turns golden brown. Divide between 4-6 metal tins. Set aside and let them cool.
2. In a bowl, mix the eggs, remaining erythritol, lemon zest, and vanilla. Add the almond milk and beat again until well combined.
3. Pour the custard into each caramel-lined ramekin and place them into a deep baking tin. Fill over the way with the remaining hot water. Bake at 345 °F for 45-50 minutes. Using tongs, take out the ramekins and let them cool for at least 4 hours in the fridge. Run a knife slowly around the edges to invert onto a dish. Serve with dollops of whipped cream, scattered with mint leaves.

**Nutrition Info:**

- Info Per Servings 1.7g Carbs, 7.6g Protein, 26g Fat, 269 Calories

## Strawberry Vanilla Shake

Servings: 4

Cooking Time: 2 Minutes

**Ingredients:**

- 2 cups strawberries, stemmed and halved
- 12 strawberries to garnish
- ½ cup cold unsweetened almond milk
- 2/3 tsp vanilla extract
- ½ cup heavy whipping cream
- 2 tbsp swerve

**Directions:**

1. Process the strawberries, milk, vanilla extract, whipping cream, and swerve in a large blender for 2 minutes; work in two batches if needed . The shake should be frosty.
2. Pour into glasses, stick in straws, garnish with strawberry halves, and serve.

**Nutrition Info:**

- Info Per Servings 3.1g Carbs, 16g Protein, 22.6g Fat, 285 Calories

## Coco-ginger Fat Bombs

Servings: 10

Cooking Time: 10 Minutes

**Ingredients:**

- 1 cup coconut oil
- 1 cup shredded coconut
- 1 teaspoon erythritol
- 1 teaspoon ginger powder
- ¼ cup water

**Directions:**

1. Add all ingredients and pour ¼ cup water in a saucepan on the medium-low fire.
2. Stir constantly for 10 minutes.
3. Turn off and scoop small balls from the mixture.
4. Allow to set in the fridge for 1 hour.

**Nutrition Info:**

- Info Per Servings 2.2g Carbs, 0.5g Protein, 12.8g Fat, 126 Calories

# Tips to be energized every day

1. Morning Exercise: Start with a quick workout.

2. Stay Hydrated: Drink water for alertness.

3. Balanced Nutrition: Eat protein, fats, and carbs.

4. Short Breaks: Stretch and breathe.

5. Positive Affirmations: Boost your mindset.

6. Power Naps: A quick recharge.

7. Sunlight Exposure: Mood and rhythm.

8. Deep Breathing: Stress reduction.

9. Socialize: Connect for energy.

10. Declutter: Organize for focus.

# MEASUREMENT CONVERSIONS

## BASIC KITCHEN CONVERSIONS & EQUIVALENT

### DRY MEASUREMENTS CONVERSION CHART

3 TEASPOONS = 1 TABLESPOON = 1/16 CUP

6 TEASPOONS = 2 TABLESPOONS = 1/8 CUP

12 TEASPOONS = 4 TABLESPOONS = 1/4 CUP

24 TEASPOONS = 8 TABLESPOONS = 1/2 CUP

36 TEASPOONS = 12 TABLESPOONS = 3/4 CUP

48 TEASPOONS = 16 TABLESPOONS = 1 CUP

## METRIC TO US COOKING CONVERSIONS

### OVEN TEMPERATURE

120℃ = 250° F

160℃ = 320° F

180℃ = 350° F

205℃ = 400° F

220℃ = 425° F

### OVEN TEMPERATURE

8 FLUID OUNCES = 1 CUP = 1/2 PINT = 1/4 QUART

16 FLUID OUNCES = 2 CUPS = 1 PINT = 1/2 QUART

32 FLUID OUNCES = 4 CUPS = 2 PINTS = 1 QUART = 1/4 GALLON

128 FLUID OUNCES = 16 CUPS = 8 PINTS = 4 QUARTS = 1 GALLON

### BAKING IN GRAMS

1 CUP FLOUR = 140 GRAMS

1 CUP SUGAR = 150 GRAMS

1 CUP POWDERED SUGAR = 160 GRAMS

1 CUP HEAVY CREAM = 235 GRAMS

### VOLUME

1 MILLILITER = 1/5 TEASPOON

5 ML = 1 TEASPOON

15 ML = 1 TABLESPOON

240 ML = 1 CUP OR 8 FLUID OUNCES

1 LITER = 34 FL. OUNCES

### WEIGHT

1 GRAM = .035 OUNCES

100 GRAMS = 3.5 OUNCES

500 GRAMS = 1.1 POUNDS

1 KILOGRAM = 35 OUNCES

## US TO METRIC COOKING CONVERSIONS

1/5 TSP = 1 ML

1 TSP = 5 ML

1 TBSP = 15 ML

1 FL OUNCE = 30 ML

1 CUP = 237 ML

1 PINT (2 CUPS) = 473 ML

1 QUART (4 CUPS) = .95 LITER

1 GALLON (16 CUPS) = 3.8 LITERS

1 OZ = 28 GRAMS

1 POUND = 454 GRAMS

## BUTTER

1 CUP BUTTER = 2 STICKS = 8 OUNCES = 230 GRAMS = 8 TABLESPOONS

## BUTTER

1 CUP = 8 FLUID OUNCES

1 CUP = 16 TABLESPOONS

1 CUP = 48 TEASPOONS

1 CUP = 1/2 PINT

1 CUP = 1/4 QUART

1 CUP = 1/16 GALLON

1 CUP = 240 ML

## BAKING PAN CONVERSIONS

1 CUP ALL-PURPOSE FLOUR = 4.5 OZ

1 CUP ROLLED OATS = 3 OZ 1 LARGE EGG = 1.7 OZ

1 CUP BUTTER = 8 OZ

1 CUP MILK = 8 OZ

1 CUP HEAVY CREAM = 8.4 OZ

1 CUP GRANULATED SUGAR = 7.1 OZ

1 CUP PACKED BROWN SUGAR = 7.75 OZ

1 CUP VEGETABLE OIL = 7.7 OZ

1 CUP UNSIFTED POWDERED SUGAR = 4.4 OZ

## BAKING PAN CONVERSIONS

9-INCH ROUND CAKE PAN = 12 CUPS

10-INCH TUBE PAN =16 CUPS

11-INCH BUNDT PAN = 12 CUPS

9-INCH SPRINGFORM PAN = 10 CUPS

9 X 5 INCH LOAF PAN = 8 CUPS

9-INCH SQUARE PAN = 8 CUPS

# RECIPES

**DATE**

| RECIPES | | | | |
|---|---|---|---|---|
| **RECIPES** | | Salads | Meats | Soups |
| **SERVES** | | Grains | Seafood | Snack |
| **PREP TIME** | | Breads | Vegetables | Breakfast |
| **COOK TIME** | | Appetizers | Desserts | Lunch |
| **FROM THE KITCHEN OF** | | Main Dishes | Beverages | Dinners |

## INGREDIENTS

## DIRECTIONS

## NOTES

| SERVING | ☆☆☆☆☆ |
|---|---|
| DIFFICULTY | ☆☆☆☆☆ |
| OVERALL | ☆☆☆☆☆ |

# Recipe

From the kicthen of ........................................................................

Serves ................. Prep time ................ Cook time ................

☐ Difficulty       ☐ Easy       ☐ Medium       ☐ Hard

# Ingredient

........................................................  ........................................................
........................................................  ........................................................
........................................................  ........................................................
........................................................  ........................................................
........................................................  ........................................................

# Directions

........................................................................................................
........................................................................................................
........................................................................................................
........................................................................................................
........................................................................................................
........................................................................................................

# APPENDIX : RECIPES INDEX

Printed in Great Britain
by Amazon

37209538R00059